SUSAN SARANDON:

A TRUE MAVERICK

by
Betty Jo Tucker

HATS
OFF™

Other books by Betty Jo Tucker:

Confessions of a Movie Addict (2001)

Susan Sarandon: A True Maverick

Published by Hats Off Books™
610 East Delano Street, Suite 104, Tucson, Arizona 85705 U.S.A.
www.hatsoffbooks.com

International Standard Book Number: 1-58736-300-3
Library of Congress Control Number: 2004090353

Cover design: Summer Mullins
Cover photo: © Stephanie Berger. All rights reserved.

ACKNOWLEDGMENTS

Susan Sarandon: A True Maverick would not have been possible without the valuable help and support I received from the following people:

Diana Saenger and Sandy Scoville, two motivators extraordinaire;

Larry Tucker, my encouraging husband;

Augusto Odone, co-founder of The Myelin Project;

Alex Friend, scientific writer for The Myelin Project;

Jacqueline Kinlow, director of development and public relations for The Myelin Project;

Chris Baker, Mack Bates, and Nathaniel Rogers, three of the world's most avid Susan Sarandon fans;

Joanna Ney, director of public relations for the Film Society of Lincoln Center;

Summer Mullins, Alex Gildzen, Stephanie Berger, Claire Folger, and J. Nathan Simmons, who all have an eye for beauty;

and a host of film critics willing to share their movie reviews.

Although the interviews I had with Brad Silberling, Barry Bostwick, Brooke Adams, Lynne Adams, and Susan Sarandon were for articles appearing on the ReelTalk Movie Reviews website, responses from each of them added significantly to the content of this book. I appreciate their candor and cooperation. My sincere thanks to all these terrific folks!

DEDICATION

Because he's such an amusing movie pal and loving husband, I happily dedicate this book to Larry Tucker.

DONATION

Susan Sarandon gave one of her most powerful performances as Michaela Odone in *Lorenzo's Oil,* a movie based on the true story of parents who refused to give up when doctors told them there was no hope for their ailing son. I am pleased to donate my author's royalties for *Susan Sarandon: A True Maverick* to The Myelin Project, a multi-national organization formed to support research on diseases like the one depicted in that inspiring film.

"Actors are the keepers of the dreams."

—- Susan Sarandon

TABLE OF CONTENTS

TRUE/FALSE QUIZ

1. Susan Sarandon keeps her Oscar on a nightstand by her bed. **T / F**

2. Director Tim Robbins originally wanted Meryl Streep for the role of Sister Helen Prejean in *Dead Man Walking.* **T / F**

3. Sarandon named daughter Eva after legendary stage actress Eva LeGallienne. **T / F**

4. *Ishtar* is Sarandon's pick as the comedy she would most like to watch when she gets the blues. **T / F**

5. Sarandon thinks the perfect dinner party guests would be Buddha, Joe DiMaggio, William F. Buckley, and Virginia Woolf. **T / F**

6. While serving as a special representative for the United Nations, Sarandon visited Afghanistan and China. **T / F**

7. In *The Witches of Eastwick*, Michele Pfeiffer got the role Sarandon was first hired to play. **T / F**

8. Sarandon studied her craft at the Lee Strasberg Actors Studio in New York City. **T / F**

9. Actor Chris Sarandon is Susan's cousin. **T / F**

10. Filmmaker Brad Silberling spent months trying to persuade Sarandon to play "Jo Jo" in *Moonlight Mile.* **T / F**

11. Author/screenwriter Gore Vidal is Sarandon's uncle. **T / F**

12. Sarandon persuaded Geena Davis to do a nude scene in *Thelma & Louise.* **T / F**

13. According to Sarandon, *Bull Durham* is her one movie that should be placed in a time capsule. **T / F**

14. Sarandon received her first Academy Award nomination for *Pretty Baby.* **T / F**

For the correct answers, turn to the next page.

"Get your facts first, and then you can distort them as much as you please."

—— Mark Twain

True/False Quiz Answers

All fourteen statements are FALSE. To discover the truth, read on.

INTRODUCTION: Why Susan?

"Be not too tame neither, but let your own discretion be your tutor: suit the action to the word, and the word to the action; with this special observance, that you o'er-step not the modesty of nature; for any thing so overdone is from the purpose of playing, whose end is, to hold, as 't were, the mirror up to nature; to show virtue her own feature, scorn her own image, and the very age and time his form and pressure."

—Hamlet's Advice to The Players (William Shakespeare)

I both envy and admire actors. They get paid for doing what most of us would love to do—pretend to be someone else. The best ones do it so well it helps the rest of us understand who we really are. And they make acting look so easy—or, as Henry Fonda explained, they "don't let the wheels show."

As someone in love with the cinema for over half a century, I've seen many incredible performances by actors who lost themselves in their roles in order to deliver truths about what it means to be human. "I've made me disappear and I put Thomas Fowler on the screen," said Michael Caine about his Oscar-nominated role in *The Quiet American.* "I've watched it three times and I look for me in there and I'm not there—nothing, not even my walk, which is quite idiosyncratic," he told Bruce Kirkland of the *Toronto Sun.* And that's why anyone who watches Caine's riveting performance comes away with greater insight about love, jealousy, despair, and compassion.

1

Judy Garland became Dorothy in *The Wizard of Oz* and rein-
forced our universal longing for home. Jack Nicholson was the lonely widower who taught us there's life after retirement in *About
Schmidt*. Frances McDormand showed us the value of persistence
when she became the dedicated pregnant police chief in *Fargo*. Tony
Shalhoub inhabited the heart and soul of the obsessed Italian master
chef in *Big Night*, thereby enlightening us concerning how frustrating
the need for perfection can be. Aaron Eckhart's metamorphosis into
the manipulative Chad for *In the Company of Men* clearly demonstrated the evils of chauvinism. Morgan Freeman and Tim Robbins
ceased to be movie stars by changing into unconventional prisoners
who helped us celebrate the virtue of patience in *The Shawshank
Redemption*. And there are many more examples of actors making us
forget they are acting. "Acting is the one art you cannot be caught
doing," declares drama coach Tony Ron.

Susan Sarandon would probably agree. Most of her performances exemplify this philosophy. That's one of the reasons she makes
such a great subject for this book.

But it's not the only reason. Mentioning Sarandon's name in
almost any conversation will perk things up considerably. People
have differing opinions about her unconventional lifestyle, her political beliefs, her many causes, and her movies. Outspoken, controversial, and extremely talented, this beautiful actress has become an
American icon, one with influence throughout the world. During her
30 years in the movies, Sarandon has portrayed some of the most
memorable female characters of the silver screen. So far, she has
earned five Oscar nominations and won the coveted golden statuette
for her brilliant work as Sister Prejean in *Dead Man Walking*.

At 56 years of age, she's still going strong. Witness her important
roles in three movies during 2002 as well as her plans to play the legendary Bette Davis in an upcoming telefilm for Arts &
Entertainment and to co-star in a 2004 film musical, *Romance and
Cigarettes*, with James Gandolfini and Kate Winslet.

When asked to write about a film star for a new series of books
focusing on celebrities, I quickly agreed. As a confirmed movie
addict, I love going to movies, discussing movies, writing about

movies. I believe movies are the central art of our time. They bring music, writing, acting, and photography together in a feast for the eyes, the intellect, and the emotions. Even while writing this, I can't wait to get my next film fix. I identify with author Gore Vidal's statement (in *Screening History*) when he observed that as he looked back on his life he realized the only thing he ever really liked to do was go to the movies.

Naturally, I'm disappointed sometimes, but going on these make-believe journeys while sitting in a darkened movie theater usually makes my endorphins kick into high gear. I agree with entertainment journalist Diana Saenger, who points out (in *Everyone Wants My Job: The ABCs of Entertainment Writing*) that the power of film makes us laugh, cry, or get angry. "Movies are probably the most influential medium in our world," she declares. "They showcase our history, offer us escapism, and become part of our everyday lives... Films guide us in how to think and behave."

As I mentioned in my last book, *Confessions of a Movie Addict*, I enjoy movies primarily for their entertainment value, but I also look forward to being enchanted by cinematic artistry, enlightened by a great story, and inspired by brilliant performances. Selecting Susan Sarandon as the subject of this book seemed quite appropriate to me. She's an actress who has demonstrated her cinematic artistry by giving brilliant performances—and most of the time in films with great stories. Coincidentally, *Atlantic City*, the movie that earned Sarandon her first Academy Award nomination, is the first film I reviewed as a critic. However, I didn't want to do a traditional biography. Marc Shapiro already wrote one (*Susan Sarandon: Actress–Activist*). Instead, I opted to present impressions of Sarandon's achievements and values from a film critic's perspective. I also decided to compile, to my knowledge, the world's first complete annotated Susan Sarandon filmography. Enjoy!

CHAPTER ONE
Recognizing a Maverick

"It's always been not only the duty but the natural place of artists—because they're outside of society—to comment on, to question, to make people look at things, to challenge their perspective on anything—not to get an answer necessarily but to reformulate the question... An informed populace is better the more information you have. The more diversity of opinion, the harder it is to control them."

—Susan Sarandon (during her 2003 Australia visit)

Wearing a slinky, spaghetti-strap black dress, her famous red hair flowing in all directions, Susan Sarandon looked every bit the glamorous movie star while gliding across the stage to accept her Maverick Award at the Taos Talking Picture Festival 2002. By the time the tribute to this Oscar-winning actress was over, any doubts I harbored about why Sarandon was selected for this award were gone.

Of course, I knew Sarandon's credentials as a great American actress were impeccable. Her Oscar for *Dead Man Walking* and her four other Academy Award nominations attest to that. And I was aware of the challenging roles she usually selected—roles that offer a different model of the Hollywood superstar. But up to this point, the term "maverick" wasn't something included in my description of this gorgeous actress. However, I realize now it's a perfect title for Susan Sarandon.

"This is so cool!" she said in her acceptance speech. "My friends are here; my daughter, who's also appearing in a movie screening at the festival is here; and I'm receiving this tribute. But when I heard about the Maverick Award, I wasn't sure what that meant, so I looked it up. I found out there really was a Mr. Maverick. He refused to brand his calves. Now, we don't know why he refused. Was he ornery? Or lazy? Or maybe he didn't want to hurt his calves. Anyway, the term maverick now means a person who doesn't conform. Well, maybe I am a bit of a maverick."

Sarandon's nonconformity is evident in the type of challenging roles she's chosen during her 30-year film career. She prefers playing strong but imperfect women who find themselves in extraordinary circumstances. Like Sarandon herself, what these characters do is at great cost. Among my favorite Sarandon performances are her roles in *Bull Durham*, *The Client*, *Thelma & Louise*, and *Dead Man Walking* (which earned her an Oscar.)

"I love making films with people who have a passion for their stories," Sarandon declared. "That's why I decided to do *Moonlight Mile* for director Brad Silberling." In this poignant drama, Sarandon portrays a woman who lost her daughter in a random act of violence. "How could I not play this part, especially after meeting the real woman my character is based on?" she asked.

In her private life, Sarandon also reveals an independent spirit. Not many movie stars will risk going to jail for their convictions. An avid human rights activist, Sarandon once joined a protest over the shooting of an unarmed immigrant by four policemen and was arrested for disorderly conduct. To back up her political and philosophical convictions, she supported Ralph Nader in his bid for the U.S. presidency and serves as a goodwill ambassador for UNICEF.

Sarandon expressed delight at being among the award recipients at the 2002 Taos Talking Picture Festival, which included independent filmmakers John Sayles and Maggie Renzi, the duo responsible for such acclaimed films as *Lone Star*, *Limbo*, *Matewan*, and *The Secret of Roan Innish*. Sayles and Renzi won the Festival's prestigious

Storyteller Award. Because they are motivated to explore different film genres while tackling relevant issues with a high level of integrity, their films deal honestly with such issues as strikes, unions, social class, and prejudice. "They inspire me with their passion for stories, and it's really an honor to be here with them," declared Sarandon, who joined the ranks of such previous Maverick Award honorees as Dennis Hopper, James Coburn, Ben Johnson, Anjelica Huston and Elizabeth Taylor.

Never one to ignore current affairs, Sarandon concluded her acceptance speech with a plea for artists to use their creativity in promoting negotiation of peace through non-violent means. "Justice without revenge," she shouted—like the true maverick she is.

In addition to her Maverick Award in 2002, Sarandon received a similar honor from the First Amendment Center and the Nashville Independent Film Festival. She was named the year's Freedom in Film Award winner for her powerful combination of professional and personal commitment to free expression and civic activities.

Sarandon, of course, has more going for her than a Maverick image. With her impressive acting talent, she's managed to maintain a longstanding film career—which reminds me of a birthday card I received not too long ago. The message? "Remember, you're not just getting older. Like the Mona Lisa, you're becoming more valuable." Flattering, I know, but definitely more appropriate for someone like Susan Sarandon, a seasoned actress who has displayed remarkable staying power in a business where glamour and youth seem necessary for success.

Along with Sarandon, the list of notable actresses who exemplify what I call the "Mona Lisa Factor" includes Anjelica Huston, Maggie Smith, Judi Dench, Goldie Hawn, Sigourney Weaver, Kathy Bates, Catherine Deneuve, and many others. Huston's recent portrayal of an Irish widow left to raise a family in *Agnes Browne* (which she also directed) is a memorable one—a performance combining both her dramatic and comedic ability. Smith continues to wow audiences with her humorous characterizations in films like *Gosford Park* and the *Harry Potter* series. Dench still commands the screen in diverse roles ranging from "M" in the latest James Bond flicks to the snobbish Lady Bracknell in *The Importance of Being Earnest*. Hawn looks as perky as ever in *The Banger Sisters*; Weaver convinces everyone that a much younger man would fall for her in *Tadpole*; and Deneuve's classic beauty shines through in *8 Women*. In *About Schmidt*, Bates proves her incredible acting chops are growing even stronger. These mature thespians are masterpieces of inspiration for women of any age.

According to Sarandon's agent Martha Luttrell, her client's work stands out by reaching both men and women. "Men find her sexy, and she's allowed a woman her age to be considered sexy," Luttrell explained to *Variety*'s Bredan Phillips while discussing Sarandon's Deauville Film Tribute. "And women admire her role as a mother and activist. Also, she has a comfort about her age; she doesn't try to be something she isn't."

Mack Bates, Arts and Entertainment Editor for Film at *The Leader* (a University of Wisconsin student newspaper) and avid Sarandon fan writes, "The woman is the best actress alive, hands down. She can take an ordinary part and imbue it with a welcome kinetic and sassy quality completely of her own design. It's as if she were capable of transcending gender to become a life force—even though no one in their right mind would ever question the fact she is all woman."

Sure, Sarandon can act up a storm, but perhaps the roles she accepts have contributed to her endurance in filmdom. Consider Sarandon's choices during 2002, a year in which she brought three very different "mature" characters to life on the big screen.

In *Moonlight Mile*, "Jo-Jo" and her husband (played by Dustin Hoffman) have suffered the loss of a daughter killed in a random act of violence. Sarandon and Hoffman portray the grieving mom and dad with excruciating realism. Sarandon's Jo-Jo faces each day using sarcasm and a biting wit to hide her deep sorrow. One critic hit the nail on the head with her insightful description of Sarandon's performance. Patty Miller-Marshall of *The Popcorn Chronicles* wrote, "Sarandon played the role with enough irony to keep the tragedy from defining Jo-Jo. A writer, she was one of these people who can barely contain her need to describe what she sees in blunt and vivid terms. It's often too much honesty for those who confuse trite, scripted dialogue with conversation. After the loss of her child, there was no comfort in words so she preferred that people said nothing. Her writer's block paralleled the empty space that was growing around her, threatening to pull what remained of her life into the vacuum of despair."

Sarandon said simply, "I consider this role a continuation of *Dead Man Walking* [her Oscar-winning performance], showing a person going from a dark place to the light and not landing on revenge."

The role of "Mimi" in *Igby Goes Down* stretched Sarandon's range by giving her the chance to play a demanding woman dying of cancer who must deal with an incorrigible young son. Although portraying an unsympathetic role, Sarandon endows this complex character with a bit of humor and lots of style. According to Sarandon, Mimi lacks spirituality as well as competence as a mother. But despite her faults, the woman's two sons have inherited her ability to survive and her sense of humor. Sarandon calls Igby "one of the truly original films to come out recently."

In *The Banger Sisters*, Sarandon and Goldie Hawn are two aging groupies who rekindle their friendship after 20 years apart. Sarandon's "Lavinia" has turned over a new leaf and wants to forget her past. Now married to a wealthy lawyer, she has two teenage daughters played by Erika Christensen and Eva Amurri (Sarandon's real-life daughter who is a riot in a very funny role here), does charity work, and always wears beige. When the free-spirited Suzette (Hawn) shows up in a colorful and outrageously sexy outfit, Vinnie refuses to welcome her with open arms. Sarandon makes Vinnie seem very real as she changes from an uptight suburban mom to the swinger of her earlier days. "This film might have been a bit more frivolous," she declared, "but it has themes important to explore."

Sarandon sums up her roles in 2002 by explaining, "These women were all very different, but similar in that they were mothers who succumbed to certain temptations. And all three movies were labors of love."

Even before 2002, Sarandon wasn't afraid of playing obnoxious roles. She told Mack Bates why such parts appealed to her in an interview about *Anywhere But Here*. "I like portraying people who have a lot of faults," she said. "If you get into that icon realm and you don't keep a sense of humor about yourself, it can be really destructive to you personally and to your craft because you get atrophied and you can't exercise all those other muscles... It's like if you don't dance for a while and you get up to dance and all of a sudden you're self-conscious."

While talking with Paul Fischer of *Film Monthly* about the challenge of acting, Sarandon discussed more details concerning her personal approach and admitted to using all her wild and varied experiences as part of the process. "That's what's so great about acting, because you use everything as opposed to an orthodontist who is stuck with his angst," she said. "You do it without design, surviving, making right choices, bringing some dignity to your work, having a sense of humor, evolving as a person, as you stay in this business ending up at 70 not bitter and alcoholic. That's the challenge."

Sarandon also explained to Fischer about how deeply she gets into each character she plays. "Forget about walking in somebody else's moccasins," she said. "You're in their house; you're in their clothes; you're in their head; you're in the lives; and when you do that, it can all be reduced to what do people need. They want to be loved; they're afraid of dying; they want to reach out."

Displayed on Daily Celebrations.com, a provocative quote from Sarandon reveals her positive attitude about her profession. "To me, the whole point of acting is to experiment and learn—it's like being hundreds of lives in one lifetime. Actors are in a privileged position, being able to create something that affects people and challenges their perspectives. Actors are the keepers of the dreams."

Sarandon views acting as an exploration of the human psyche. If she hadn't chosen to be an actor, she might have become a psychologist. Alan Lovell, Media Studies Lecturer at Staffordshire University, believes Sarandon's opinions about acting coincide with those expressed by the great Russian teacher/director Constantin Stanislavsky. In *Screen Acting* (Routledge Press), Lovell writes, "She defines good acting in what are clearly Stanislavskian terms: 'If you're working with people who really listen and try different things and invent a lot and are very specific, it can be wonderful. It's just about listening and being specific.' From such a perspective, there are two key acting challenges. The first is to give performances a sense of freshness and spontaneity. This is achieved by the actress 'listening' to her fellow actors, not coming to her performance with prepared responses. In line with this, Sarandon often emphasizes the importance of remaining 'open' in a scene. The second challenge is to give your character a strong sense of individuality. This is achieved by inventing responses that are 'specific' to your character."

Lovell continues, "Sarandon isn't a Method actress. In creating her characters, she is more dependent on the script than Method performers typically are. Again and again in discussing her performances she refers to the quality of the script. To support her reading of it, she generally uses naturalistic methods. In *White Palace*, she put on weight because she thought it was appropriate for the character she was playing. In *Lorenzo's Oil* she got to know the couple the story was based on and modeled her performance on Michaela Odone. Because of her emphasis on the script, Sarandon often suggests changes when she feels a script isn't working... Sarandon's emphasis on the script also means that dialogue is of great importance and forms another reference point in her discussions of acting. She defined one of the main challenges in *Bull Durham* as 'handling language' and 'speaking all those words.'"

Explaining why he responds so strongly to Sarandon's performances, Lovell writes, "In the first place, Sarandon's work is marked by an expressive energy. She consistently finds strong and varied physical movements, gestures, and facial expressions to define the characters she plays. She demonstrates the same kind of vocal energy: lines are shaped and pointed so that they have maximum effect. Crucially, this expressiveness is combined with intelligence and this is what marks Susan Sarandon out for me. Energy alone isn't enough; it can produce undisciplined, over-the-top performances. Nor is her technique outstanding—there are other actresses who have equal or stronger techniques. But again and again in watching her performances, I have been struck by the sense that the choices she has made are the right ones...they are based on a deep understanding of the dramatic context she is working within...and the human context to which the dramas refer."

Personally, I'm impressed by the way Sarandon gets straight to the heart of her characters, endowing them with dramatic individuality while paying close attention to the way each one interacts with other characters in the movie. (Bette Davis got it right when she observed, "The real actor has a direct line to the collective heart.") More concerned about the truth of a feeling than how it's projected, Sarandon excels at acting for the camera, which can pick up the tiniest flicker of false emotion. She observes and listens well. I think Stanislavsky would be proud of her. In *An Actor Prepares*, he advised actors who want to be real artists to lead a full, interesting and exciting life as well as to study the life of people around them. "We need a broad point of view to act," he wrote.

Besides developing the qualities mentioned above, Sarandon brings an appealing physical appearance to the big screen. First of all, there's that stunning red hair. I don't know why, but there's something fascinating to me about redheaded actresses. I felt Maureen O'Hara, with her flaming mane, exemplified the beauty of Technicolor back in the 1940s, and I never missed one of her flicks. Imagine my surprise while doing research for this book when I came across something called the "ginger gene," which is supposedly responsible for fair skin and red hair. According to the Red and Proud website, when it emerged in ancient times, it was frequently suppressed because of fear and superstition. The Egyptians buried redheaded children alive; the Greeks believed having red hair indicated mental instability.

Nowadays, we're more civilized—it's just easier for redheads to get noticed, especially a redhead like Sarandon who's also blessed with a lovely figure and a distinctive turned-up nose. Still, for me, it's her large, almost pop-out eyes that express so much and make me care about the characters she portrays. By looking into those incredible eyes, we can see the inner strength of Sister Prejean in *Dead Man Walking*, the vulnerability and intelligence of Reggie Love in *The Client*, the gut-wrenching determination of Michaela Odone in *Lorenzo's Oil*, the blatant sensuality of Annie Savoy in *Bull Durham*, the old-fashioned innocence of Janet Weiss in *The Rocky Horror Picture Show*, the self-absorbed pride of Celimene in *Illuminata*, the poignant toughness of Jo-Jo in *Moonlight Mile*—to cite only a few examples.

When I asked Sarandon to name her all-time favorite roles during a telephone interview, Sarandon laughed and replied, "That's like asking me to choose my favorite child. I loved *Moonlight Mile* and am disappointed it didn't get a wide release. Maybe when the video comes out, people will find it. And I had a blast doing *Bull Durham*, but *Igby Goes Down* gave me the chance to work with a great ensemble. Still, I just loved working on *Moonlight Mile* with Dustin [Hoffman] and Jake [Gyllenhaal]. Jake and I stay in touch and giggle and carry on. It was great to be on that set in my comfy socks and all."

In an interview for MSN.com, Sarandon elaborated on her *Moonlight Mile* chemistry with Hoffman. "He's not somebody that made me defensive," she stated. "He's very open, and I don't think he was threatened by me, so we didn't have to do that dance. We didn't have to settle in... He's very cuddly, and we just had a basis of respect. There's no accounting for it. He's a good family man, and I'm a family person, so that probably bonded us to each other." (Is there any truth to the story about Sarandon and Hoffman meeting for the first time and sharing a shower at auditions for *Kramer vs. Kramer*? Maybe, but I haven't been able to verify it. No eyewitnesses!)

Brad Silberling, writer/director of *Moonlight Mile*, also shares Sarandon's concern about the limited release of that film. "We only made it to 425 theaters," he said in a telephone interview.

Why? I asked.

"It's simple and rather heartbreaking," Silberling explained. The movie had been given a greenlight at Touchstone Pictures by an executive who was a strong supporter of the project. But three days before *Moonlight Mile* wrapped, that person left and another VIP, who was not enthused about the film, took over. "But a different company owns overseas distribution rights, and I think we will do very well there," Silberling added. He also praised Sarandon's performance in

Moonlight Mile as "amazing" and probably feels considerable gratitude about her behind-the-scenes efforts.

When Sarandon realized that Silberling's movie might not be released at all, she took an unfinished version with her to the Taos Talking Picture Festival. Positive audience reaction there helped prevent that wonderful movie from being shelved.

Observing Sarandon at the Taos Festival, I marveled at her high energy level. How does she keep up such remarkable physical and emotional strength? "I don't have a secret," she said in our telephone conversation. "I never feel like I'm doing a good job. I always think I'm over-extended, but I just haven't learned how to say no—and sometimes I think the people who criticize me for not concentrating on one thing might be right. I'm always juggling balls and some are dropping as we speak."

Having just returned from Australia and New Zealand, Sarandon sighed over the piles of catch-up work waiting for her. "I have a 10-year-old and a 13-year-old at home, so I want to give them as much attention as possible," she declared. Admitting she's lucky to be blessed with good health, Sarandon added, "Although I do work out, it's not the Madonna type of exercise. But I try to keep in shape. And living in New York, I'm on foot a lot."

Because Sarandon was fortunate to inherit a slender body type, she had to gain 20 pounds to play the voluptuous waitress in *White Palace*. "I was always a skinny, skinny kid," she told Mack Bates in *The Leader* interview. "I was in college and couldn't get over 100 for the longest time. I just couldn't gain weight for anything." Whatever she's doing now, it works for her. Movieline Magazine gave Sarandon the "Most Shockingly In Shape for a 50+ Woman Award" in its 2002 "100 Most" list.

Sarandon reminds me of great actresses in the past who worked successfully after 50. She combines the charisma of Joan Crawford with Maureen O'Hara's feistiness and Bette Davis's on-screen authority. I can imagine her doing *Mildred Pierce*, *The Little Foxes*, and *The Quiet Man* with equal aplomb. In fact, Sarandon admitted to Sheryl Altman of Women.com that she longs for the days "when actresses did it all"—comedy, drama, musicals, romance. She named

Katharine Hepburn, Myrna Loy, and Carole Lombard (all three were mavericks in their own right) as actresses who moved effortlessly between projects without anyone thinking twice about it. "There isn't as much flexibility in Hollywood for women today," she observed. "If you're a type, they want you to stay a type."

It's not surprising a maverick like Sarandon refused to opt for playing only one type of role during her 30-year acting career. Filmdom is richer for that decision.

"I love making films with people who have a passion for their stories."

—Susan Sarandon

CHAPTER TWO
Balancing Act: Family and Career

"I have found the best way to give advice to your children is to find out what they want and advise them to do it."

—Harry Truman

I first saw Susan Sarandon in person at the back of a darkened theatre. She was graciously receiving compliments about her daughter's performance in *Made-Up*, one of the movies shown at the Taos Talking Picture Festival 2002. Eva Amurri (named after Eve—"the first woman to get a bum rap," explains Sarandon), whose big expressive eyes resemble those of her mother, was absolutely charming in this hilarious coming-of-middle-age comedy directed by Tony Shalhoub. Eva plays a teenage wannabe cosmetologist who performs an elaborate makeover on her mother (Brooke Adams). The complicated beautifying process includes a tape-on facelift, eye tucks, and a wig. Her mother's sister (Lynne Adams) documents the transformation for a video class she's taking.

Finding the right person to play the teenage daughter was proving to be extremely difficult, according to Lynne Adams, who also produced the movie. Auditions were held in Boston and on the West Coast, but a week before shooting began the role was still not cast. Tony liked one person, Brooke another, and Lynne a third, but there

Susan Sarandon's daughter, Eva Amurri, and star Brooke Adams in Made-Up, *directed by Tony Shalhoub. Photo: Claire Folger. Courtesy of Sister Films ©2001.*

was not one they could agree on. "I ran into Eva while shopping in New York," Brooke told me. "And I thought she looked gorgeous. Susan and I have been friends for years. I was at the hospital when Eva was born, but I hadn't seen her for a long time. As soon as I saw her, I thought she would be perfect for the role." Brooke said Susan put Eva on tape for an audition and was very happy with Eva's part in the film. "She was with us all during filming and made some good suggestions, but never came across as a 'stage mother.'"

Lynne said, "Eva was absolutely great, just delightful. She knew her lines letter perfect. She's funny, mature, believable, down-to-earth—not a stage brat." Because Eva was only 15 when she did *Made-Up*, Sarandon and her daughter shared a B&B during the filming. "I think it was good for Susan and Eva to have this time together, away from the guys," Lynne stated. The result? Eva holds her own among an experienced cast that also includes Shalhoub and Gary Sinise.

Later, Sarandon bragged to me about Eva's other 2002 flick. "She has talent and I admire her fearlessness, the way she makes fun of herself in *The Banger Sisters*"—a comedy in which Sarandon played Eva's film mom. On March 29, 2003, the Young Artists Association agreed with Sarandon by giving Eva its Best Supporting Young Actress in a Feature Film Award for her hilarious portrayal of the spoiled brat in *The Banger Sisters*.

Sarandon has every right to be proud of her daughter's acting ability. But she also wants Eva to explore other options. "Eva's just gone through the process of applying to college, so she'll get a peek into other things," Sarandon explained. "She's planning on studying something besides drama, maybe languages." Still, Sarandon admits to helping Eva with advice about how to find an agent and the business side of Hollywood. According to the candid mom, "It's the only time I knew anything that she didn't know."

And Sarandon spoke highly of Eva's upcoming film *Saved*. "It stars a great group of young actors: Macaulay Culkin, Jena Malone (my daughter in *Stepmom*), Mandy Moore. It's set in a Christian high school, and it's a satire." Eva portrays Cassandra, an adamantly Jewish girl targeted for conversion by religious zealot Moore. Although dealing with important topics like religion and ethics, *Saved* is billed as dark comedy.

In an interview with Andy Dougan for the online *Evening Times*, Sarandon talked about how much she enjoyed working together with Eva in *The Banger Sisters*. "She's so beautiful and has this incredible body and way of holding herself, and she threw it all away and became this kind of gangly, whining, hysterical comic relief," Sarandon said.

Has Sarandon ever advised her daughter against going into show business? That's the question Bonnie Laufer asked Eva in a *Tribute*

"Star Chat" about *The Banger Sisters*. "I think in the very beginning she was very cautious if only because this business involves a lot of rejection," the up-and-coming young actress replied. "It's really easy to get hurt by it. But I think she understands that this does not easily hurt me, and she is behind me 100 percent. She understands this is what I want to do and she supports it."

How does Sarandon manage to balance her family and career so effectively? She surprised me by saying that being a movie actress sometimes helps her be a more organized parent. "Actually, I get rest when I'm working on a film. I have a driver, cooked meals and so forth."

Sarandon likes to make films in New York, where she and her family live. She began taking her children on the set when they were very young, and daughter Eva appeared in Sarandon's films at an early age. She played Sister Prejean as a 9-year-old in *Dead Man Walking*. With that kind of exposure to an acting career, it's no surprise Eva wants to follow in her mother's footsteps. She knows first-hand the rewards as well as the challenges involved.

Sarandon tries to encourage 18-year-old Eva, 14-year-old Jack, and 11-year-old Miles no matter what their interests are. "The only thing that really made me nervous about raising kids was having a privileged kid who wasn't interested in anything," she explained during the 2002 Toronto International Film Festival. "If they have a passion, I'm there—because I don't know how you deal with the other."

On the lighter side, Sarandon admits to embarrassing her kids a lot. As reported on the Susan Sarandon unofficial fan site, she insists, "That's my job. You never quite know when you're going to make them cringe. One moment it's okay to kiss them in front of school and the next afternoon it's like heresy. My daughter will leave out clothing for me for the entire week because I'll go to the gym and never get out of my sweats. I remember once we were going to some awards show, and she looked at me and went 'You're not going out like that'—so everything embarrasses them at a certain point."

Sarandon scored points with Eva by introducing her to Leonardo DiCaprio at the *Man in the Iron Mask* premiere. "I felt like a complete sleaze trying to get Leo to meet my daughter," she confessed. "I kind of weaseled my way down to where he was standing and I got my daughter and six of her friends down there, too. Thank God Leo gave me a big hug and talked to the girls for 15 minutes."

Because Sarandon herself is the oldest of nine children, I suspect a strong motivation accounts for much of her success as a mother. Having babies later than most mothers also seems a plus for her. According to the *National Enquirer*, she even jokes about being the "Patron Saint of Older Women's Ovaries." The Internet Movie Data Base lists this telling quote under Sarandon's mini-biography: "If I was 22 and trying to build a career, I don't know who'd be watching the kids as happily as I do. It takes so much to get me to break out of my domestic paradise. There's hardly anything that interests me as much as my family."

Does Tim Robbins, Sarandon's longtime significant other and father of her two sons, play a key role in that domestic paradise? You betcha. It's rumored he even gets up in early in the morning when Sarandon wants to sleep in and fixes breakfast for the kids. And that sometimes he helps Sarandon entertain them by singing along and dancing to "You're the One That I Want" from the *Grease* soundtrack (Susan Sarandon and Tim Robbins in *Grease*? Now there's something I'd pay big bucks to see!)

In 2001, Sarandon described a "Day in the Life of Susan Sarandon" (posted on the Susan Sarandon Site), a personal account illustrating her dedication to her children and Robbins. "During term time I walk my kids to school," she explains. "Then I'll go to the gym. I often don't get around to changing out of my gym clothes. My daughter Eva will lay outfits out on the bed and plead for me to change. Having kids is a big priority for me. I thought I couldn't have children, but I had Eva when I was 39 and Miles at 45. My kids haven't seen my movies. They're not interested. They like me as me. Since I've been a special representative for UNICEF, I've been traveling without them. They hate UNICEF because I'm gone. I leave them token presents for every day I'm away: a baseball card, a lipstick, chocolate. I bribe them!

"Tim and I have been very productive since we've been together. It's easier when one person does the creativity and the other takes care that 'real life' happens smoothly. But when two people work out-side the home and have artistic temperaments and needs, and both are powerful, that's harder to figure out.... I guess we travel a lot. Last summer we were in Ecuador and did the Galapagos and Bali. I trust in travel more than formal education: seeing how other people live humbles you. When I'm in India for UNICEF, I don't get much sleep. At 5:30 a.m. it will be dinnertime at home in New York, so I'll call the kids. Then I'll eat breakfast—tea, scrambled eggs and toast and rice—while watching the sun come up."

Sarandon clearly relishes being a mother. Even though she knew taking time off to have children could mean losing her career, she had no qualms about it. She adores her kids.

Maybe that explains why she willingly takes on so many "movie mom" roles. Sarandon has played all kinds of mothers—good ones, bad ones, outrageous ones—starting way back in 1978 in the role of a prostitute with a beautiful young daughter (Brooke Shields) in *Pretty Baby*. Most actresses in their early thirties avoid appearing as some-one's on-screen mother, but Sarandon followed *Pretty Baby* the same year with *King of the Gypsies*, a film in which she was cast as the moth-er of Eric Roberts. She's well on her way to becoming the "mother of all film moms" with stellar performances in the films already men-tioned as well as in *Little Women, Lorenzo's Oil, Safe Passage, Stepmom, Igby Goes Down, The Banger Sisters*, and *Moonlight Mile*. According to Sarandon, mothers have always been played in movies like there's one kind of mother. "I'm striving to make these roles more than just 'mothers'—but also real women."

Sarandon claims she hasn't forgotten what it's like to be an ordi-nary person. "I don't feel any different than I did before I started making movies and became recognizable. I still do my laundry, I take care of my kids... I haven't become isolated." Like most ordinary people, family comes first for her.

CHAPTER THREE
Roles of Distinction

"You get what you settle for."

—Louise Sawyer in *Thelma & Louise*.

Although Sarandon appeared in 57 movies (including TV films) from 1970 through 2002, I think her most unforgettable performances emerged in *Atlantic City*, *Bull Durham*, *The Client*, *Thelma & Louise*, and *Dead Man Walking*. Playing a wannabe croupier opposite Burt Lancaster's old-time hood in *Atlantic City* (1980) earned Sarandon her first Oscar nomination as well as widespread critical acclaim. Lancaster and Sarandon complemented each other with their age difference and in-depth portrayals of two poignant characters—and Sarandon finally achieved recognition as a serious actress, which her campy earlier work in *The Rocky Horror Picture Show* had caused some critics to doubt. About her *Atlantic City* performance, the late, great film critic Pauline Kael wrote, "Her double takes are very delicate; she keeps you tuned in to her feelings all the time." (This from someone who complained earlier about Sarandon's "googly eyes and slightly stupefied look.")

Surprisingly, even after her sensational work in *Atlantic City*, Sarandon had to campaign shamelessly for the role of a seductive baseball groupie in *Bull Durham* (1988). Granted, between those two fine movies came such career lows as *Compromising Positions* and *The Buddy System*. After persuading the studio heads and director Ron Shelton to meet with her about portraying the sexy Annie Savoy, Sarandon used her own funds to pay for a flight from Rome to Los Angeles. Appearing at the interview in a skin-tight dress, she won the all-important role as Kevin Costner's co-star. Why was Sarandon so motivated to go after this part? "Annie was smart, sexy, spacey, funny, and poetic," she explained to Bob Costas after taping of his HBO *On the Record* show about *Bull Durham*'s 15th Anniversary. "You find one role for a woman like that maybe every 10 years or so, if you're lucky." Fortunately, portraying Annie Savoy served as more than a boost to Sarandon's career. It also did wonders for her love life. While working on this flick, Sarandon met Tim Robbins, the handsome young actor who later became her long-time partner.

With *Thelma & Louise* (1991), Sarandon scored points for feminists everywhere with her no-nonsense portrayal of a brassy waitress who shoots the man attempting to rape her best friend (Geena Davis). In an interview for Syd Field.com, screenwriter Callie Khouri (whose screenplay won an Academy Award) described how she came up with the plot for this unusual film. "When I got the idea 'two women go on a crime spree,' I felt this strange sense of euphoria," she wrote. "I didn't want to write about two stupid women or two evil women who go on a crime spree. I wanted to write about two normal women.... There's a side of you that you really don't know exists. And you don't know what the trigger for it is. You think you're a normal person and you have a normal life. That kind of tenuous relationship we have with our normal life was really intriguing to me. How one little thing can happen and your whole world falls completely apart."

Playing the protective Louise, Sarandon added to her reputation as a dramatic actress by receiving a third Oscar nomination. Davis earned a nomination, too, thereby dividing the final vote—so neither Louise nor Thelma took home the little golden guy that year. Although the Oscar went to Jodie Foster (for *Silence of the Lambs*), *Thelma & Louise* became a landmark film, mostly because of memorable performances by Sarandon and Davis, who both made the cover of *Time* magazine.

Disappointed, of course, at not winning the Academy Award, Sarandon nonetheless seemed intrigued by the controversy surrounding the film's depiction of two gun-toting female friends. She refers to the film as "a cowboy movie with gals and trucks instead of trucks and horses" and told the *Los Angeles Times*, "I don't think we understand how firmly the heterosexual white male was holding onto that territory of heroic movie maleness."

In contrast to actively campaigning for a role in *Bull Durham*, Sarandon was vigorously sought after to star in the film version of John Grisham's novel *The Client* (1994). I understand Grisham wrote the character of far-from-perfect attorney Reggie Love with Sarandon in mind. In addition, director Joel Schumacher believed she would be just right in the part. He actually got down on one knee and pleaded with her to join the cast. Fortunately, Sarandon finally agreed. She brought "Reggie" to life on screen as a character magnificent to behold—intelligent, combative, and vulnerable. To me, this performance ranks as Sarandon's best.

Next, wonder of wonders, a frumpy Sarandon sans make-up or any semblance of glamour emerged in *Dead Man Walking* (1995) and waltzed away with the Academy Award as Best Actress of the year. Although the film presents a balanced look at the issues surrounding the death penalty, Sarandon herself holds strong views against legalized executions. Speaking out against the death penalty at her Deauville tribute, she declared, "It's costlier; it's capricious; it's arbitrary; it doesn't deter crime."

Sarandon's humanistic portrayal of Sister Helen Prejean, a real-life nun who empathizes with both the killer and the victim's families, was a powerful spiritual revelation for movie fans. In a 1995 interview with Alan Moroney, Sister Prejean described how she first met Sarandon. "She was in Memphis filming *The Client* and someone gave her a copy of my book. She had to come to New Orleans for two days of filming, so she called me and said, 'I'm reading your book and I'm always interested in substance of character, so I'd like to meet you.' So I met her in a restaurant and we began to talk and I really liked her because I knew I had to find really trustworthy people to do a film of my book. You know I wasn't real anxious for Hollywood to do it. 'Well,' she [Sarandon] said, 'I really think Tim would be interested in producing, directing, and making this film. Let me bring him the book,' which she did."

Bemoaning her character's lack of even a touch of mascara, Sarandon claims portraying Sister Prejean "purged me of any sense of vanity." *Dead Man Walking* also gave Sarandon another opportunity to work with Tim Robbins, who agreed to adapt Sister Prejean's book for the screen and serve as the film's director. Happily, despite some stormy moments, the Sarandon/Robbins personal relationship survived their close professional collaboration on *Dead Man Walking*. In her Oscar acceptance speech, Sarandon thanked Robbins for being her "best partner in crime."

Upon completion of *Dead Man Walking*, Sarandon helped Robbins by taking on one of her most surprising roles and creating a gem of a supporting performance in his *Cradle Will Rock*, a film about trying to mount a controversial play in New York during the 1930s. Her portrayal of Margherita Sarfatti, Mussolini's mistress, may have shocked some of her liberal friends and colleagues, but Sarandon told Annlee Ellingson (of Boxoffice Online), "I've played lots of people that don't have my politics; your job as an actor is to suspend your judgment to a certain extent and to care about them and understand what they do."

Margherita, a patron of new painters in Italy, came to the U.S. to sell Mussolini to the American people. "In the context of the film," explained Sarandon, "she's somebody who has a job to do and because she loved art, she sometimes finds herself giving art away to people she feels don't really appreciate it." Sarandon names *Cradle Will Rock* as one of her favorite New York movies. "It's great to see a part of New York's theatrical history and see a glimpse of life in the theatre at that time," she says.

In recognition of her many outstanding performances, Sarandon has been nominated for and received numerous awards. Here's the impressive list:

Academy Awards: 5 nominations (*Atlantic City*, *Lorenzo's Oil*, *Thelma & Louise*, *The Client*, *Dead Man Walking*); one Oscar (*Dead Man Walking*).

BAFTA Awards: 2 nominations (*The Client*, *Thelma & Louise*); one win (*The Client*).

Blockbuster Entertainment Awards: 2 nominations (*Dead Man Walking*, *Stepmom*); one win (*Stepmom*).

Boston Film Festival: winner of the 1992 Film Excellence Award.

David di Donatello Awards: 2 nominations for Best Foreign Actress and 2 wins (*Thelma & Louise*, *Dead Man Walking*).

Emmy Awards: 2 nominations for Outstanding Guest Actress in a Comedy Series ("Malcolm in the Middle" and "Friends").

Genie Awards: winner of 1981 Genie for Best Performance by a Foreign Actress (*Atlantic City*).

Golden Globes: 5 nominations for Best Performance by an Actress in a Motion Picture Drama (*White Palace*, *Thelma & Louise*, *Lorenzo's Oil*, *Dead Man Walking*, *Stepmom*); 1 nomination for Best Performance by an Actress in a Motion Picture Comedy/Musical (*Bull Durham*); 1 nomination for Best Performance by an Actress in a Supporting Role in a Motion Picture (*Igby Goes Down*).

Golden Satellite Awards: 1 nomination for Best Performance by an Actress in a Leading Role (*Stepmom*).

Gotham Awards: winner of the 1992 Actor Award.

Hasty Pudding Theatricals: 1996 Woman of the Year Award

Kids' Choice Awards: winner of the Blimp Award as Favorite Voice in Animated Movie (*Rugrats in Paris: The Movie*).

Las Vegas Film Critics Society Awards: winner of the 2002 Sierra Award for Best Supporting Actress (*Moonlight Mile* and *Igby Goes Down*).

National Board of Review: co-winner (with Geena Davis) of 1991 NBR Award for Best Actress (*Thelma & Louise*).

San Diego Film Critics Society Awards: winner of 1998 Best Actress Award (*Stepmom*).

San Sebastian International Film Festival: winner of 1995 Donostia Lifetime Achievement Award.

Screen Actors Guild Awards: 2 nominations for Outstanding Performance by a Female Actor in a Leading Role (*The Client*, *Dead Man Walking*); 1 win (*Dead Man Walking*).

Venice Film Festival: winner of 1982 Posinetti Award for Best Actress (*Tempest*).

Women in Film Crystal Awards: winner of 1994 Crystal Award.

In 2002, Sarandon earned a well-deserved star on the Hollywood Walk of Fame, along with fellow actors Martin Scorsese, Robert Duvall, and Kevin Bacon. Her star is right next to Whoopi Goldberg's. And Sarandon was honored at a Gala Tribute by the Film Society of Lincoln Center during 2003. Scheduled soon after the cancellation of the Baseball Hall of Fame *Bull Durham* 15th Anniversary Celebration (because of statements against the Iraqi war by Sarandon and Robbins), many fans feared this tribute might face the same fate.

"There were some people who were unhappy," Joanna Ney, public relations director for the Lincoln Center Film Society, admitted in a telephone conversation. "But we were not honoring Sarandon for her politics; we honored her for being a brilliant actress—and it was a great night."

The Film Society of Lincoln Center has celebrated the work of a major film artist annually since 1972. Sarandon joined the ranks of such previous honorees as Alfred Hitchcock, Barbara Stanwyck, Charlie Chaplin, Audrey Hepburn, Clint Eastwood, Billy Wilder, Frederico Fellini, Alec Guinness, Elizabeth Taylor, Al Pacino, Fred Astaire, Mike Nichols, Bette Davis, Gregory Peck, and Francis Ford Coppola.

Susan Sarandon with Irene and Bernard Schwartz at her Gala Tribute given by the Film Society of Lincoln Center at Avery Fisher Hall on May 5, 2003. Photo: Stephanie Berger © 2003. All rights reserved.

Among those taking the podium to give testimonials for Sarandon at the 2003 Gala were actors Tim Curry, John Turturro, David Bowie, and Geena Davis, who confessed she actually wanted to play Louise, not Thelma. "However, by dissolving in a puddle of admiration around Susan, I found myself becoming Thelma," Davis explained.

Turturro talked about how much he admired Sarandon's acting and praised her amazing longevity and improvement with age. Curry told a funny story about how he met Sarandon in a health food store. "And this was before the L.A. fitness craze," he stated. "She was talking about going to a trapeze class because, as she explained, 'If I'm going to work out, I may as well learn a new skill.'"

Sarandon's family came along with her. Tim Robbins was there as well as their two pre-teen sons, Jack Henry and Miles Guthrie. Eva

Amurri, Sarandon's teenage daughter, also accompanied her. Referring to the clips being shown, Sarandon said, "My children haven't seen these movies." (Most of the films feature mature content.) Then she smiled, shrugged her shoulders, and sighed, "Oh well."

Nathaniel Rogers of FilmExperience.net, who attended the New York Gala, wrote, "It was moving to see someone so courageous and outspoken celebrated at this point in time. Susan Sarandon is so beautiful live." Rogers reported that the night ended with Sarandon graciously thanking the crowd after receiving a standing ovation and declaring how lucky she was to have a profession that's such a perfect fit for her.

Sarandon claims she "fell into acting by accident." She has no formal acting training. Although she received a college degree in drama from Catholic University in Washington, D.C. (where she also took courses in English, philosophy, and military strategy), her studies involved the theater from a literary perspective. So how did she get into the acting game? Sarandon answered that question in her 2002 interview with Paul Fischer for *Film Monthly*. "I went to an audition with my then-husband who was trying to get an agent, and he needed someone to do a scene with him, which we did, and they said 'Why don't YOU act?'"

After the audition, Sarandon accompanied husband Chris in his summer stock work. When they came back in September, she got a part in *Joe*, a movie filmmakers had been trying to cast for a long time. Sarandon claims she was then cast in every part she went up for. "It just kept happening," she said. "And I just started to learn what I was doing a little bit, got some craft down... I don't know if it was because I really didn't care and I really wasn't desperate, but I just kept getting things—so the next thing I know, I had a career."

Luckily, Sarandon began to love the acting craft—and still does. In addition to her movie work, she has appeared in stage productions and on television. Her theater credits include *An Evening with Richard Nixon, The Guys, A Coupla White Chicks Sitting Around Talking,* and *Extremities.* Her television appearances have been on such shows as *A World Apart, Search for Tomorrow, Sesame Street, Owen Marshall,*

Counselor at Law, The Simpsons, Mad TV, and *Friends*. She's also made the following television movies: *F. Scott Fitzgerald and the Last of the Belles, June Moon, Who Am I This Time, A.D. Anno Domini, Mussolini: The Decline and Fall of Il Duce, Women of Valor, Earthly Possessions, Children of the Dune*, and *Ice Bound*. Sarandon's voice has been heard in a number of documentaries including *The Shaman's Apprentice, AIDS: The Facts of Life, 900 Women, Uphill All the Way*, and *The Nazi Officer's Wife*. ReelTalk film critic Donald J. Levit called her narration in *The Nazi Officer's Wife* "impressive and unobtrusive."

Maintaining a sense of humor about all her awards, Sarandon keeps her Oscar statuette in her bathroom. Speaking to the audience at her Cape May Film Festival tribute, she announced facetiously, "I'm going for a rest stop. I have all my other awards, but I want a rest stop named for me." That doesn't surprise me. Sarandon's quirky humor also comes out in her choice of the comedy she would like to see most when she gets the blues. The Susan Sarandon Site reports that it's *Waiting for Guffman*, Christopher Guest's hilarious mockumentary about amateurs putting on a show. Her selection of "perfect dinner partners" (as listed on the same website) also makes me smile. Just imagine the excitement generated by Sarandon and her four "ideal" guests—Jesus Christ, Gore Vidal, Edward Albee, and hockey player Mark Messier. And her reaction to being named the Ten of Hearts in *NewsMax's* Deck of Weasels evokes shades of Oscar Wilde. "I am elated to know there were enough people to make a full deck," she told *People* magazine.

"She [Sarandon] was the first trooper to come into my film... She cared so much about it and about her performance. She made all of us feel like a family."

—Brad Silberling, director, *Moonlight Mile*

CHAPTER FOUR
Her Colleagues Speak Out

"Without friends no one would choose to live, though he had all other goods."

—Aristotle

F ans may wonder what Susan Sarandon is like to work with. According to Julia Roberts, Sarandon's *Stepmom* co-star, who presented the Maverick Award to her at the Taos Talking Picture Festival 2002, "Susan is amazing, gorgeous, honest, remarkable, and a great artist." Roberts said much the same thing earlier in comments to *Entertainment Weekly*. "In our discussions in rehearsal—which can be really involved and really lengthy—I found her insight incredibly valuable and really interesting. She's a wonderful actress. I respect her as a friend and as a part of my tribe."

Many of Sarandon's other colleagues speak highly of her. To Barry Bostwick, who co-starred with Sarandon in *The Rocky Horror Picture Show*, she's "a real professional." Although nervous about singing in that film, Sarandon "stepped up to the plate and delivered," Bostwick (originator of the Danny Zuko role in Broadway's *Grease*) told me. "She's so competent and confident; she watches and listens and does it—she's such a natural talent." Bostwick and Sarandon knew each other before appearing in *The Rocky Horror*

Julia Roberts calls friend Susan Sarandon to the stage for her Maverick Award at the 2002 Taos Talking Picture Festival. Photo: Larry Tucker.

Picture Show. "In fact, we auditioned together," Bostwick explained. "We were sent up by the casting agent, a good friend of mine. He said, 'You guys would be perfect together. So we went—and got the parts." Bostwick mentioned how difficult making this film turned out to be. "It was a low budget flick," he pointed out. "There were no dressing rooms, so if you had to go to the bathroom, you headed for the bushes." (No wonder Sarandon caught pneumonia during filming.) When asked if he would like to work with Sarandon again, Bostwick exclaimed, "I'd relish it!"

Brad Silberling, director of *Moonlight Mile*, also expressed his delight with Sarandon when she accepted a role in his film. "I was expecting to have to jump through the typical set of hoops. Instead, she made a commitment on the spot. She's amazing. She was the first trooper to come into my film. She cared so much about it and about her performance. She helped make all of us feel like a family. Dustin [Hoffman] told me this was the most enjoyable filmmaking experience he ever had."

Appearing at a press conference for the 2002 Toronto International Film Festival, Hoffman talked about the great chemistry between himself and Sarandon, a connection that came across so dramatically in *Moonlight Mile*. "There are other people out there in the universe that you could have been married to, married happily. I think Susan and I could have been married and could still be together," he declared. "I think I would never have won one fight with Susan," he teased.

Jake Gyllenhaal, who starred with Hoffman and Sarandon in *Moonlight Mile*, shared Hoffman's closeness with Sarandon. He told Jenny Peters of Upfront.com that he and Sarandon became great friends. "We talked and we hung out," he said. On the DVD commentary for the movie, Gyllenhaal mentions how easy Sarandon is to listen to.

In addition to helping the young actors she works with, Sarandon has assisted up-and-coming writers and directors. Burr Steers, making his film debut with *Igby Goes Down*, gives Sarandon credit for getting his project off the ground. "It was Susan agreeing that got my picture made," he said to Karen Durbin of *The New York Times*. (Steers just happens to be the nephew of Gore Vidal, a long-time friend of Sarandon's, so that probably helped considerably.) Steers told Rebecca Murray of About.com, "For me, Susan was a graduate course in making movies. She's a doctorate. Susan can do and give you anything you want in front of a camera and be incredibly effective. She's got an amazing arsenal emotionally, in her beauty and her power. She brings a palpable presence when she walks into a room and she's just incredibly kind and generous in the process."

While working on Steers's film, Sarandon made quite an impression on Ryan Philippe, who played one of her sons. In a "Star Chat" interview with Bonnie Laufer (for Tribute.com), Philippe talked about both Sarandon and Robbins, his co-star in *AntiTrust*. "They are great people, and they are incredible parents—their kids are just unbelievable—so I have learned a lot from them and their relationship, from the way they have negotiated their way through the business," he said. Commenting on Sarandon's contribution to *Igby Goes Down*, Philippe declared, "It's great to see her on the set and see how giving and how much part of the process she becomes for a big movie star. She comes to this small film, and gives everything."

In terms of "giving everything" as an actress, Sarandon certainly achieved that with her memorable performance in *Dead Man Walking*.

Tim Robbins, wearing his director's hat from that film, expressed great respect for Sarandon's acting talent. In an interview for the Charlie Rose PBS show, he said, "She's the best actress working." His comment was made in response to Rose's half-teasing inquiry concerning whether or not casting Sarandon as Sister Prejean was "automatic." When Sarandon received her star on Hollywood's Walk of Fame, Robbins stated, "She has stunned me in *Bull Durham*, *Thelma & Louise*, this morning, or when she's reading to my kids at night. Long may her star sparkle and shine!"

Robbins said much the same thing in Australia's *Herald Sun*. "We obviously have our love and trust," he stated. "So when you work with someone you love and trust it's easier. I've directed Susan three times and each time it gets easier and easier. And you know one of the things I love about her? She really has balls. She has the courage to be unsympathetic—and there are so few people who do that."

According to biographer Marc Shapiro, Geena Davis, who received help from Sarandon when she had qualms about doing a nude scene in *Thelma & Louise*, thinks of Sarandon as her role model. In his unauthorized Sarandon biography, Shapiro quotes Davis as affectionately saying, "She's crazy, strong, and out-spoken—a real troublemaker."

Natalie Portman, Sarandon's co-star in *Anywhere But Here*, shares Davis's positive feelings about her, and for similar reasons. Portman originally turned down the role as Sarandon's daughter because of requirements to do a nude scene. Sarandon insisted that casting of Portman was critical to understanding the film's mother-daughter relationship. She believed that when viewers saw the smart and healthy Portman, they would say, "Well, for all the mom's silliness and mistakes, she must be doing something right because she has such a great kid." When Sarandon refused to remain associated with the project without Portman in the cast, the script was rewritten and Portman accepted.

By the time the film wrapped, the young actress felt so secure with Sarandon that she joked about their working relationship at a press conference for *Anywhere But Here* at the 1999 Toronto International Film Festival. "She [Sarandon] is really, like, obnoxious in real life," quipped Portman, and everyone laughed. Director Wayne Wang added to the fun by saying, "They were never in the same scene together. I shot them separately. It's all in the editing, you know." Wayne also reported he cast Sarandon because he's been in love with her ever since he saw her in *Bull Durham*.

According to David Bowie, who worked with Sarandon in *The Hunger*, Sarandon is "sharp, sassy, seriously sexy—and bossy." During his tongue-in-cheek testimonial at Sarandon's Lincoln Center Gala, Bowie recalled meeting her at a reading for their movie. He admitted being nervous because he was already one of Sarandon's fans. Somehow he got up enough courage to ask her for advice. Bowie said Sarandon replied (and with great authority), "Stop acting and read the lines!"

When questioned about working with Sarandon on *The Banger Sisters*, Goldie Hawn told Kelly Carter of *USA Today*, "It's very interesting because oftentimes working with someone can ruin your relationship. The great thing is we got into script discussions early on, and that could have been the kibosh. That was the real test." Sarandon passed the test with flying colors. In an interview about *The Banger Sisters* for beatboxbetty.com, Hawn said, "Susan's great. She was very easy to work with and extremely tenacious, which I love because I can't stand people who don't follow through. She's got a very good sense of story." No wonder Sarandon and Hawn are now close friends.

Discussing his sci-fi *Children of the Dune* television series with Lisa Chambers for *TV Guide*, screenwriter John Harrison said of Sarandon (who plays the evil Princess Wensicia), "She's wonderfully collaborative. She really looks at a piece of material from the inside out. It was wonderful to work with an actress who would dig that way."

In his testimonial for Sarandon at her Lincoln Center Film Society Tribute, director Paul Schrader also commented on how deeply involved Sarandon becomes during filming. He recalled that while *Light Sleeper* scenes were being filmed, she listened so intently to other actors that she wouldn't even notice when something was going wrong and would be completely surprised when he yelled "Cut!"

In the book *Ridley Scott: Close Up*, filmmaker Scott, who directed *Thelma & Louise*, is quoted as wanting Sarandon for the role of Louise because she's "always inventive, continually surprising, and very funny." Another director, the late Louis Malle, who worked with Sarandon in *Pretty Baby* and *Atlantic City*, referred to her as "one of the very best actresses of her generation." Malle, of course, like so many men in Sarandon's life, was probably completely captivated by her.

"She is a real professional. She's so competent and confident; she watches and listens and does it—she's such a natural talent."

—Barry Bostwick, Sarandon's co-star, *The Rocky Horror Picture Show*

CHAPTER FIVE
Ah, Men!

"Well, actually no one on this planet ever really chooses each other. I mean, it's all a question of quantum physics, molecular attraction and timing. Why, there are laws we don't understand that bring us together and tear us apart."

—Annie Savoy in *Bull Durham*

I remember watching the Arts & Entertainment 1999 television Biography of Susan Sarandon and being stunned by actor Chris Sarandon's positive remarks about his former wife. Young Susan Tomalin met and fell in love with Chris Sarandon, a grad student three years her senior, while both were studying at the Catholic University Drama School in New York City. "Chris seemed to know everything because he was a graduate student," Sarandon explained. "He played a huge part in my decision to become an actress."

In 1964, after living together for three years, Susan and Chris married each other, mostly because campus officials objected to their unconventional living arrangements. (They divorced in 1968.) Ironically, Susan got hired but Chris did not when she tagged along with him to audition for the movie *Joe* (1970). Most ex-husbands aren't likely to be so complimentary. Is Chris still under her spell? Maybe not, but the marriage was based as much on mutual friendship as on love, and Chris still continues to be very proud of his ex-wife. As for Susan, she claims she was lucky to find Chris. "I thought he was responsible for my blossoming," she told Aimee Lee Ball in an interview for *Mother Jones*.

Chris is now married to actress Joanna Gleason. Although his acting career hasn't reached the heights of his ex-wife's, it's nothing to be ashamed of. He earned a Best Supporting Actor Oscar nomination for *Dog Day Afternoon*, voiced the role of Jack Skellington in *The Nightmare Before Christmas*, appeared in several films including *Protocol, The Princess Bride, Child's Play, and Fright Night*. He's also seen frequently on television series like *ER* and *The Court*.

Marc Shapiro (*Susan Sarandon: Actress–Activist*) points out that Sarandon went through a lot of changes as a result of her romance with the volatile John Leone, who directed her in *The Great Smokey Roadblock*. Because of their conflicting personalities, that relationship lasted only a short time. Sarandon sought therapy, emerging as a much tougher person.

Sarandon's romantic relationship with French director Louis Malle developed during the filming of *Pretty Baby*, but it had started to wane by the time they worked together again on *Atlantic City*. It's not difficult to understand Sarandon's attraction to Malle. She talked about Malle's exceptional filmmaking skill in a 1999 interview with Adrian Wootton of *The Guardian*. "A lot of his genius came in the editing," Sarandon explained. "He would say 'Sometimes you have to kill your darlings.' Sometimes the scene that you shot the movie for is not the scene you need any longer, and so you have to be ready to realize when the film takes on a life of its own because of who you cast, because of a happy accident, whatever it is, and go with the film you now have...and I think there is a certain amount of genius inherent in that."

Before coming to America in 1970, Malle already established himself as one of France's most versatile New Wave filmmakers. His autobiographical film about life in occupied France, *Au Revoir Les Enfants*, earned widespread critical acclaim, and he had directed such megastars as Jeanne Moreau and Brigitte Bardot. However, because Malle spent much of his time in Europe, Sarandon saw him only infrequently. Out of sight, out of mind, as the old saying goes. (Malle later married actress Candice Bergen.)

Enter Franco Amurri, the charismatic Italian filmmaker who served as an assistant director for Paul Mazursky's *Tempest* (1982). Sarandon fell in love again, and much to her surprise, since physicians had told her she could not have children, became pregnant with daughter Eva. Neither party wanted marriage, but Sarandon had no qualms about becoming an unwed mother, even though approaching her forties. Sarandon's romance with Amurri fizzled in much the same way her relationship with Malle did.

In 1988, sparks flew between Sarandon and Tim Robbins on the set of *Bull Durham*. Did it matter that Robbins was 12 years younger than Sarandon? Not a bit. Sarandon had finally met her physical, emotional, and political soul mate. The handsome 6'4" Robbins, who is nothing like the dimwitted character he portrayed in *Bull Durham*, no doubt impressed Sarandon with his intelligence and liberal social conscience. She must have been pleased to hear about Robbins graduating from UCLA with honors and subsequently joining The Gang, a drama group noted for presenting radical political observations with an avant-garde form of theater. He worked in a day-care center when he was 10, marched against the Vietnam War when he was 12, and directed his first play when he was 14. Like Sarandon, Robbins was raised as a devout Catholic. He served as an altar boy, attended a high school for gifted children, delivered pizzas to help pay for his college education, and loves hockey.

According to biographer Marc Shapiro, Robbins was "literally a mirror image" for Sarandon—a politically and socially aware individual who was not afraid to make his opinions known. "He was not somebody that Sarandon felt she would have to baby and boss around," writes Shapiro. "She felt his creative energy and passion. And much like Chris Sarandon and Louis Malle, there was a sense of individuality and self-confidence that was equally as attractive as his rugged, still boyish good looks."

Although they're not officially married, Sarandon and Robbins have remained together since their *Bull Durham* days and have two young sons, Jack Henry and Miles Guthrie. Robbins told James

Kaplan of *US*, "It's not like we're making some kind of political statement. I feel like I am married to her. We have made a long-term commitment to each other. So nothing beyond that is necessary."

Robbins said much the same thing at the Sarandon Lincoln Center Tribute. Admitting he had difficulty preparing his speech because he's protective about his relationship with her, he saluted Sarandon with "unmarried but forever committed to you."

In tune on various current issues, Sarandon and Robbins worked with each other in *Cradle Will Rock*, *Bob Roberts*, and *Dead Man Walking*. Robbins served as director on all three movies. He postponed *Cradle*, his pet project, to take over *Dead Man Walking*, a film Sarandon wanted him to helm. Another sign of Robbins's commitment to Sarandon came after the horrific September 11 terrorist attacks. When he found out all flights had been canceled, he drove from Los Angeles to New York City (a 56-hour road trip) to be with Sarandon and their children.

"The Tim Robbins Universe" fan site reports that Sarandon took Robbins to Paris for his 40th birthday. In return, when Sarandon turned 50, Robbins rented an entire resort in the Bahamas for a week and invited 50 of her closest friends to celebrate with her. Guests included Sean Penn, Robin Williams, Geena Davis, and Julia Roberts.

On the negative side, Sarandon jokes about hating the way Robbins eats his breakfast cereal. And, according to an article in Australia's *Herald Sun*, she admits being frustrated by having to play the nagging and killjoy role with their children. "He [Robbins] will play long into the night with them," she explained. "I'm the one who says, 'It's time to come in now, it's getting late.' And he can play for hours. Sometimes he has to remind me that I should forget about it and join in the game." Still, because someone has to make sure the kids do their homework and say no sometimes, Sarandon believes she and Robbins are a good match as parents.

Another potential problem area relates to Robbins's protective attitude. Consider his telephone call to Sarandon's mother after she told a reporter of her concerns about the grandchildren being brainwashed by their parents. Lenora Tomalin declared, "It left me devastated." Unfortunately, Robbins verbally attacked the same reporter at an Oscar night party, resulting in some very bad press.

Will the Sarandon/Robbins relationship last? Sarandon looks at this question realistically. She told Paul Fischer of *Film Monthly*, "Some day my family will be off on their own and then we will have to look at our empty nest and see where we stand with that.... I know many people at this stage of their lives that are going through a difficult situation because their priorities have changed. Who they are has not necessarily changed but become clearer, and they no longer need a guy to be the one doing this or that, and they no longer need wives to do things, and they have to re-evaluate.... They have to find some new way for their relationship to work."

In August of 2002, Robbins and Sarandon appeared together again professionally. They traveled to Scotland to participate in the Edinburgh Festival Fringe as co-stars of *The Guys*, a play about the heroic firemen who were involved in saving victims of New York's September 11 terrorist attack. Sarandon played a New York professor of journalism who helped a fire department captain (Robbins) with eulogies in a memorial service for eight colleagues who died as a result of rescue efforts at the World Trade Center.

According to Tom Peterkin (writing for news.telegraph.co.uk), Sarandon seemed pleased to be working with Robbins again. "It's probably what's saving us," she confessed. "We're still together as a couple because we respect each other as actors and I respect Tim as a writer." No one watching the 61st Annual Golden Globes Awards in January of 2004 could doubt that respect. In Sarandon's televised introduction of *Mystic River*, one of the Best Drama nominees, she absolutely glowed with pride over Robbins's Best Supporting Actor win for his exceptional work in the very film she was presenting.

In her professional life, because of her ability to project a smoldering sexuality, Sarandon has created some unforgettable on-screen moments with many of her leading men. She's certainly co-starred with some of the best, including Burt Lancaster, Dustin Hoffman, Kevin Kline, Barry Bostwick, John Turturro, Jeff Goldblum, Nick Nolte, Sam Shepard, Jack Nicholson, Robert Redford, Paul Newman, and Gene Hackman. Who can forget the famous "pedicure" scene between Kevin Costner and Sarandon in *Bull Durham*? Or the explosive sexual chemistry between Sarandon and a much younger James Spader in *White Palace*? To me, those film moments rank right up there with romantic scenes between such perfect screen partners as Cary Grant and Ingrid Bergman, Glenn Ford and Rita Hayworth, Katharine Hepburn and Spencer Tracy, or Humphrey Bogart and Lauren Bacall. Writing for *Script* magazine, Diana Saenger observed about the last pair, "The sensual tension between them always started with just a spark, a certain look or some clever word play, but soon ignited into a forest fire of passion." That kind of chemistry is hard to define, but it reminds me of Mark Twain's observation, "Words are only painted fire; a look is the fire itself."

Still, I think Sarandon's most dynamic rapport with male co-stars emerged, ironically, in two performances that lacked her trademark sensuality. As Reggie Love in *The Client*, she and Tommy Lee Jones complimented each other so perfectly in their adversarial roles I forgot I was watching a film. And as Sister Prejean in *Dead Man Walking*, the intense connection between Sarandon and Sean Penn as a condemned convict and his spiritual counselor almost overwhelmed the film's dramatic story. (Those rumors about Sarandon becoming pregnant with Penn's child during filming? Not true, she says.)

Mae West once announced she preferred two types of men—domestic and foreign. Sarandon also appears to prefer two types of men—actors and directors. Fortunately, Tim Robbins is both.

CHAPTER SIX
The Myelin Project

"If an elderly but distinguished scientist says that something is possible, he is almost certainly right, but if he says that it's impossible, he is very probably wrong."

—Arthur C. Clarke

Because of her remarkable performance in *Lorenzo's Oil* (1992), a movie about parents trying desperately to find a cure for their ailing son, Sarandon earned another Oscar nomination. She played Michaela Odone, Lorenzo's mother, opposite Nick Nolte, who portrayed Augusto Odone, her husband and Lorenzo's father.

"She was able to seize the spirit of my late wife," said Augusto in a telephone interview. "And there was a physical resemblance. She seemed to have the same 'tiger mother' instinct."

When Lorenzo was five years old, he began doing strange things like bumping into objects. Augusto and Michaela soon received the horrifying news that their son had a rare, incurable genetic disorder that would cause him to lose all his bodily functions and die before he reached his teens. This disorder, known as adrenoleukodystrophy (ALD) only affects boys, but it's passed on through the mother. The Odones refused to look at this illness as incurable, so they began doing research on their own. After two years of fighting with the

51

Michaela Odone (left) and Susan Sarandon, who portrayed her in Lorenzo's Oil. *Photo courtesy of The Myelin Project.*

medical establishment and parents of other ALD boys, they discovered a blend of plant oils they thought would help their son.

Explaining her deep feelings for Michaela to Gavin Smith of *Film Comment*, Sarandon said, "I just see her as becoming primal in her clarity in protecting and watching over Lorenzo... She is so uncompromising and so pure. The depth of her energy is just astounding."

Commenting to Smith regarding critic David Denby's complaint about her "unsympathetic" portrayal of Michaela, Sarandon declared, "Michaela was very pleased, so I don't care what Denby thinks." Even though Sarandon claims the role of Michaela is the furthest one from who she really is, Michaela and Sarandon grew to be friends, and Sarandon even invited her to attend the Oscars.

Sarandon now serves as spokesperson for The Myelin Project. "She's extremely nice to work with," Augusto declared. "She has no hang-ups. Most people do, but she doesn't. She says what comes into her mind. She's very frank. She has some kind of inner force, and people listen to her.

"I started the project with Michaela ten years ago," explained Augusto. "It has made some inroads, not only among scientists. All doctors admit freely that with The Myelin Project, research has been accelerated. Researchers tend to be prima donnas, but they are collaborating now instead of competing."

Information on The Myelin Project website describes an organization clearly worthy of Sarandon's support. Its goal is to accelerate research on myelin repair. Myelin, the white matter insulating the nerves, allows the conduction of impulses from one part of the body to another. It can be destroyed by hereditary neurodegenerative disorders, such as the leukodystrophies, and by acquired diseases such as multiple sclerosis. All together, demyelinating diseases affect an estimated one million people in the industrialized countries alone.

Behind The Myelin Project is a multinational gathering of families struck by one demyelinating disease or another. Refusing to accept the conventional view that science cannot be hurried, they resolved to advance the moment when myelin could be restored. They have done this by creating a framework in which researchers can cooperate effectively, by giving scientists adequate, prompt financing, and by continuously interacting with them. To counter researchers' endemic conservative stance, The Myelin Project personnel constantly remind them of two aphorisms: "Fortune favors the brave," and "You never know until you try."

Inspired by great projects of the past (like Project Apollo) which used a motivating time-conscious approach to attain specific goals, The Myelin Project has set up a Work Group from among the top international laboratories specializing in myelin repair. With the Apollo Project, the moon was the objective. With The Myelin Project, remyelination is the objective. The impressive Work Group includes researchers from Yale University, Mount Sinai Medical Center, and the University of Wisconsin at Madison in the United States, The Intituto Superiore di Sanita and San Raffaele Scientific Institute in Italy, the College de France, L'Hopital de la Salpetriere and the Institut Pasteur in France, the Queen's University at

Kingston in Canada, the University of Cambridge in the United Kingdom, and the Max Planck-Institut in Germany.

My admiration for Augusto and Michaela (who died of lung cancer in 2000) knows no bounds. Although not medical doctors, they developed a therapy now adopted on both sides of the Atlantic that reverses the biochemical defect of ALD. And they did this while facing the skepticism of doctors, scientists, and support group members. Who could believe that a substance developed by two lay people would be able to halt the deadly disease? Some people called the Odones "quacks." They were certain that Lorenzo survived only because of the excellent care he received.

Fortunately, a 10-year-long trial conducted by Dr Hugo Moser (played by Peter Ustinov and depicted unfairly in the film) proved that boys who were not given the oil "scrupulously" were almost three times as likely to develop symptoms as boys who were given it without fail. Dr. Moser concluded that the oil, while not a preventive treatment, clearly lessens the chances of suffering from the symptoms. Amazing! An oil made up of fats extracted from olive oil and rapeseed oil emerged as a near miracle.

According to Lucy Atkins of *The Guardian*, when research proved Lorenzo's oil really worked, Augusto said, "I already knew it worked"—and then described a scene from the movie showing some young boys, all with the ALD, jumping up and down. "I knew those children," he told Atkins. "I put them on Lorenzo's oil. I have followed those children as they are growing up. None that I know of have got the disease."

In her article, Atkins explained how it is thought Lorenzo's oil works. "It affects the 'very long chain fatty acids' in the boys' bodies," she wrote. "In boys with ALD, the enzyme that breaks down these fatty acids is impaired. They can't properly metabolise these acids, which then build up and begin to damage the central nervous system. Specifically, they destroy myelin—the white matter that insulates the nerves and allows impulses to be conducted from one part of the body to another." Atkins pointed out that this is why some early signs of ALD involve memory loss, emotional instability, and vision/hearing/motor problems. "Usually, boys who have the childhood form of ALD will be bedridden, blind, and unable to swallow by the age of 10. They will die soon after," she concluded.

The Myelin Project headquarters are in the Washington, D.C., metropolitan area, the location of NIH and other sophisticated research facilities, and one of the world's principal centers for medical research. The Myelin Project has branches in Britain, France, Germany, Italy, Switzerland, and Dubai. Neither Project president Augusto nor members of the board receive compensation. The Myelin Project targets its funds toward clinically oriented experiments on the cutting edge of remyelination research. Basic research and studies directed toward the advancement of science for science's sake are excluded from Project financing.

Three main strategies have been adopted by The Myelin Project to achieve its objectives: prompting researchers to work as a team and coordinating their research efforts; promoting interaction between researchers and lay people, and rapid financing of practically oriented experiments.

"From now on, I'm only interested in research to help humans," Augusto said in our telephone conversation. "To some extent, what I have succeeded in doing is to stop forms of basic research instead of practical research."

As of June 2002, The Myelin Project had financed 29 experiments for a total of approximately $4,000,000. The year of 2001 marked a turning point for The Myelin Project, when Schwann cells were transplanted into the brain of an MS patient for the first time in medical history. Currently, several other promising research projects await funding.

Financing experiments is only one of the Project's features. As Dr. Ian Duncan, one of the Work Group's scientists, stated in an interview with *People* magazine, "The Myelin Project has given us more than money...it has given us inspiration...added a focus to our work and has provided us with a human context."

On May 29, 2003, Lorenzo Odone celebrated his 25th birthday. Although deprived of most of his functions, his mind is still active. Lorenzo blinks his eyelids to communicate "no" and says "yes" by wiggling his fingers. He likes being read to and listening to music. He also enjoys receiving mail from well-wishers—which can be sent to him in care of The Myelin Project, 2136 Gallows Rd., Suite E, Dunn Loring, Virginia 22027 U.S.A.

According to Augusto, the real value of *Lorenzo's Oil* (the movie) has been "to show people that in cases where you have a disease in the family or yourself, you have to be proactive."

Commenting further on the power of the movie, Augusto reports that many science teachers from around the country have written to him about showing the film to their classes. As a result, a teaching kit was developed. It contains a copy of the film, an outline of a study guide, a slide show about how Lorenzo's oil works, and a CD of the song "Lorenzo" sung by Phil Collins. Augusto believes that teachers realize how valuable the movie is—not only as a teaching tool—but also as a way to motivate students to continue their interest in science after completing high school.

Jacqueline Kinlow, director of development and public relations for The Myelin Project, reports receiving 500 requests for the teaching kit during 2003. "It's not only science teachers who are interested," she said. "Many professors of ethics, philosophy, and other humanities courses want their students to learn they can make a difference in this world. And they seek to enliven the imaginations of their students through use of our teaching materials."

Lorenzo's Oil shows the power of movies to change lives for the better. On my list, it's right up there with *A Slender Thread* and *Pay It Forward* in terms of social impact. All three films have inspired people to get involved in activities to help others. After seeing Sidney Poitier's portrayal of a college student volunteering at a crisis center and watching his unselfish and dedicated efforts to prevent a caller's suicide in *A Slender Thread*, I—like many viewers throughout the nation—participated in setting up a local Crisis Hotline. *Pay It Forward*, although spoiled for me by its unsatisfactory ending, created quite an impact with its theme of doing good deeds for three individuals and expecting them to do the same for three others who each help three others, and so on. Catherine Hyde Ryan, author of the book upon which the film is based, has even set up a foundation offering grants to programs designed to help young students realize they can change the world. The Pay It Forward Foundation also provides them with opportunities to do so.

Films like these serve as a welcome antidote to the relentless car chases, violent action sequences, and mind-numbing special effects emphasized in so many current movies.

CHAPTER SEVEN
Her Critics Speak Out

"For an actress to be a success, she must have the face of a Venus, the brains of a Minerva, the grace of Terpsichore, the figure of Juno, and the hide of a rhinoceros."

—Ethel Barrymore

Although Sarandon won the 1998 ShoWest Humanitarian Award and receives praise from individuals all over the world for her involvement in numerous social causes, she's no stranger to negative criticism. Just ask the hosts of *The View*, who might think twice before inviting her back after a guest appearance in which she blasted them for being more interested in gossip than in politics. She told the women they should be considering things like "what's happening in Burma with civil rights" instead of "what's allegedly happening to poor Winona Ryder."

Or talk to Gil Cates, producer of the 1993 Academy Awards television show. That was the year Sarandon and Robbins presented the Oscar for Best Film Editing, and then called attention to the plight of 250 AIDS-stricken Haitains held at Guatanamo Bay in Cuba. Cates had warned the couple not to make any political statements during their presentation. Ignoring that warning, Sarandon and Robbins were booed by some members of the audience. In *Susan*

Sarandon: Actress–Activist, biographer Shapiro mentions that Cates was livid. "For someone who I invite to present an award to use that time to postulate a personal political belief I think is not only outrageous, it's distasteful and dishonest," he said.

Sarandon and Robbins were also criticized for supporting Ralph Nader's presidential campaign in the 2000 election. Many loyal Democrats believed (correctly) that most votes for Nader would come from Democrats, thus insuring a Republican win. Others thought Sarandon's outspoken campaigning would hurt her career, but that didn't happen.

Although Sarandon took an anti-war stance against George Bush's plans for Iraq by accusing him of hijacking "our losses and our fears" after the 9/11 terrorist attacks, she bristles when called unpatriotic. "I'm tired of being labeled anti-American because I ask questions," she told reporters in London at the premiere of *The Banger Sisters*. She also complained about Prime Minister Tony Blair's support of Bush, according to Valerie Mass, reporting for the *Denver Post* (January 30, 2003), which probably rankled a few Brits.

As an anti-war protestor during U.S. involvement in Vietnam, I understand Sarandon being upset when people think she doesn't love this country. "Peaceniks" were suspect back then, too. I remember my job as a college dean being in jeopardy as a result of hiring the famous pacifist poet Daniel Berrigan to teach in the Upward Bound program. Those were troubled times, and calling fellow citizens "traitors" for harboring different opinions about military action didn't help solve anything then—nor will it now.

Sarandon's speech for the October 2002 anti-war rally in Washington D.C.—in which she expressed fear for Iraqi children—evoked many negative responses from Internet visitors to a website called Small Victory. One person wrote, "You're afraid for Iraqi children? Unlike your children, who enjoy the spoils of your riches every day and lead pampered lives, the children of Iraq live in fear of their brutal leader. Their lives mean nothing to Hussein. They don't expect to have a future, let alone a good one. What do you propose to do about that, Ms. Sarandon? Do you want to go over there and save each and every Iraqi child so they won't have to endure a life of fear and misery? Wouldn't it be easier to get rid of the one guy that puts the fear into their lives—their leader? No, in your world everything can be solved with a peace pipe and a handshake."

Obviously, celebrities willing to express unpopular opinions face the ire of many fellow citizens. Robert P. Laurence, writing for the *San Diego Union-Tribune* on April 18, 2003, reported on a VH1 survey that polled 1,030 Americans about this topic. Fifty-four percent "thought it was inappropriate for celebrities to make public statements about political events." However, the results varied depending on the age of the individuals being polled. Fifty-six percent of people in the 20-29 age group indicated it was okay for celebrities to make their opinions public, but sixty-three percent of respondents over 50 didn't like the idea.

In reaction to the unpopular anti-war stance of such actors as Sarandon, Martin Sheen, Sean Penn, George Clooney, and Jessica Lange, housewife Lori Bardsley started an online petition, Citizens Against Celebrity Pundits. "We, the undersigned American citizens, stand against wealthy Hollywood celebrities abusing their status to speak for us," states the Internet document.

The *National Examiner* of February 2003 called these same stars "traitors." In an article by Art Dworken, Rev. Jerry Falwell is quoted as saying, "Their words almost make you feel they hate America." And Pat Buchanan adds, "They are basically, with all due respect, airheads and lightweights."

In the same article, Ben Ferguson, named Young American Broadcaster of 2002 by the National Association of Radio Talk Show Hosts, complains, "Through petitions, newspaper ads, rally speeches, seemingly endless sound bites on TV, even a trip to Baghdad, these showbiz traitors have been using their celebrity status to turn the minds of their fellow citizens against President George W. Bush and his administration."

Even Sarandon's mother, Lenora Tomalin, speaks critically about her daughter's anti-Bush stance. "I am a conservative. I voted for George W. Bush, and I simply agree with most everything he has said," she told syndicated columnist Lloyd Grove. "When I visit Susan, I tread on eggs," she added.

According to Scott Maxwell of the *Orlando Sentinel*, Mrs. Tomalin wasn't worried about her comments harming her relationship with her daughter because she loves Susan, knows she has always been opinionated and strong-willed and that her opinions come from deeply held beliefs. "I've never been one to talk politics with the family," Mrs. Tomalin explained. "I just voted and went about my business." Appearing on TV's *O'Reilly Factor*, Susan's mother reacted negatively to the host's labeling of her daughter as a Radical. "That's harsh," she admonished him.

Publicity surrounding this story, together with Sarandon's "peace sign" gesture as a presenter at the Oscar ceremony in March of 2003, caused quite a furor. Because of negative e-mails and phone calls, The United Way of Tampa, Florida canceled a fund-raising event where Sarandon was scheduled to be the keynote speaker. Robin Carson, chairwoman of the United Way Board of Directors, said the event had the potential to become divisive. "The focus of our whole meeting had shifted to whether or not we were creating political platform for Susan Sarandon," she explained.

A disappointed Terry Tomalin, Sarandon's brother and a writer for the *St. Petersburg Times*, had arranged for her appearance at the United Way event. His wife Kanika, a member of the 100-member women's leadership group, resigned from the committee responsible for the program. "People have a right to believe and say what they want," she said. And Marty Petty, executive vice president of Times Publishing Company (which publishes the *St. Petersburg Times*), resigned as a member of the United Way board of directors and chair of the 2003 campaign, stating that his decision was "grounded in a lifelong personal belief that our civic life is made stronger by the expression of all views, including ones that are controversial."

According to the *Toronto Star*, Sarandon's response to the United Way's action was one of disappointment and dismay. "Considering the depletion of federal funds for community programs and the faltering economy, it is disturbing to me that the United Way is letting partisanship determine its support base," Sarandon said. "Once again, the shortsightedness of the powerful will end up hurting those in need."

Caricature of Susan Sarandon by Patrick Sterno of Caricature Zone.

Concerned citizens began flooding newspapers throughout the country with "letters to the editor"—pro and con—about this and related incidents. Tom Helmantoler of Julian, California, wrote to the *San Diego Union-Tribune* (April 27, 2003), "Celebrities such as Sarandon and Tim Robbins have yet to figure out that it's the people, not the government, who've given them the backlash for their comments." Roberta Alexander of Menifee, California, echoed this sentiment in her letter printed on May 4, 2003. "Some of our celebrities and their supporters and apologists are missing the point that has made lots of people angry with them: They hijack events held for other purposes and force those present or tuning in to listen to their diatribes," she said. And Claire Marie Wachowiak of Chula Vista pointed out, "I also have the right to speak my mind and have my opinion heard. Since my platform isn't as large, I choose to do it by not supporting their movies, CDs, and TV shows. That's my right."

In that same "Letters" section, Chad Stevens, also from the San Diego area, took a different stance. "My little brother is in Iraq right now; as a result I'm emotionally tied to this issue," he wrote. "No matter how you slice it, Saddam is, was a bad person, and I'm proud to belong to a nation that stepped up and took him out. I don't share Sarandon's views. At the same time, it troubles me that she has been unable to act on her conscience without apparently excessive political fallout. She didn't go to Hanoi and ride anti-aircraft artillery. She made a polite and dignified stand for peace, resulting in public discourse on an important topic. America's ability to embrace opposition to that war is what I love about this country. It's what makes the United States the greatest nation on Earth."

An unusually creative type of criticism aimed at Sarandon came earlier from Jim Wrenn, editor of PolitSat.com. During the 2000 presidential campaign, he composed the following satirical limerick about her:

SUSAN SARANDON, POLITICAL BANTAM

When Susan Sarandon said Dubya
'has blood on his hands' as Gov'nor
'cause he executed
instead of commuting
the maximum sentence for dozens,
why didn't she also deplore
support for such laws by Al Gore?
Until she learns facts
as well as she acts
perhaps she should say less not more.

Because of their anti-Iraqi war actions, Sarandon and Robbins became persona non grata for Baseball Hall of Fame president Dale Petroskey, who cancelled the scheduled 15-year anniversary celebration of *Bull Durham* soon after the start of Operation Iraqi Freedom. "Ultimately, they could put our troops in danger," Petroskey declared. Faced with 28,000 responses in the form of phone calls, letters, and e-mails, he apologized for not contacting the couple before making his decision.

One of the complaints Petroskey received came from sportswriter Roger Kahn, author of *The Boys of Summer*, who cancelled his August Baseball Hall of Fame speaking engagement in protest. "By canceling the Hall of Fame anniversary celebration of *Bull Durham* for political reasons you are, far from supporting our troops, defying the noblest of the American spirit," Kahn wrote in his letter to

Petroskey, who once served as deputy press secretary for Ronald Reagan.

In addition to Sarandon's political activities, her lifestyle of unwed motherhood, out-of-wedlock affairs, and living with Robbins without marrying him also raised many eyebrows. It's no surprise she became the target of conservative talk-show hosts. In terms of her professional life, not every Sarandon performance has received rave reviews. Pauline Kael panned her work in *Pretty Baby*, accusing her of giving "an inexplicably petulant and vapid performance; she did so much ruminating she was cowlike."

Surprisingly, Media Studies Lecturer Alan Lovell, who admits Sarandon is his favorite contemporary movie star, complained about her acting in *Twilight*, primarily because the role she played required none of her trademark energy. "Catherine Ames is a passive iconic figure, an ageing actress whose major successes are in the past. Sarandon can bring little to such a figure, and as a result this is one of her least interesting performances," Lovell wrote in *Screen Acting* (Routledge Press).

Roger Ebert gave thumbs down to Sarandon's turn as the house-wife sleuth in *Compromising Positions*, "Sarandon is truly lost in this situation," he wrote in his review. "She ends up as more of a traffic cop, racing from one scene to another, tying the threads together. At the end, she isn't victorious, she's exhausted."

And online critic Sandy Grossman, in her Internet Movie Data Base Review of *White Palace* (filmed in St. Louis) complained, "Susan Sarandon sports a truly unusual hick accent that I never heard once while I lived in St. Louis, and I lived there 17 years."

In contrast to high praise from the Odones for Sarandon's portrayal of Michaela in *Lorenzo's Oil*, Dr. Jerri Nielsen complained about Sarandon's performance in *Ice Bound*, a CBS movie based on her book. "This isn't me," she said in a telephone interview arranged by CBS and reported by John McKay in Canada.com. Nielsen, the Ohio doctor who had to treat herself for breast cancer when stranded in Antarctica, stated, "I don't think she read my book; she didn't talk to me."

Additional criticism resulted from Sarandon and Robbins's appearance at the Edinburgh Festival Fringe in *The Guys*, a play about the brave firemen who died during the 9/11 tragedy. They were chastised by the *Telegraph* as being "smug and sanctimonious." Tim Peterkin reported that the couple had to defend themselves against charges they were exploiting the disaster—which must have hurt Sarandon deeply, considering the time she spent volunteering at Ground Zero.

No matter how much her critics speak out—some even demanding a boycott of her movies—Sarandon continues to be pursued for multiple film projects every year. Witness her three important roles in 2002 and her plans to portray Bette Davis in an upcoming telefilm announced by Arts & Entertainment network. I think Sarandon as Davis would be perfect casting. She certainly has those "Bette Davis eyes" that Kim Carnes sang about. And Davis, like Sarandon, earned a reputation as an independent spirit as well as a marvelous actress. The careers of both women are characterized by longevity and acclaim. It's my understanding that the film will focus on Davis during the time she made *All About Eve* and earned an Oscar for that role—which means the age would be about right for Sarandon. I can hardly wait to hear Sarandon deliver that famous Davis line, "Fasten your seatbelts; it's going to be a bumpy night."

In 2003, Sarandon completed *Children of the Dune*, a Sci-Fi Channel mini-series in which she played the ruthless Princess Wensicia. Describing Wensicia to Staci Layne Wilson of Myria.com, Sarandon said, "My character is just great, evil high-collared mirror-mirror on the wall [type]. Lots of hair acting. I worked with roaches, a raven, and an owl." Clearly, she thinks this role is a hoot. And *Moonlight Mile*'s Brad Silberling told me he's writing something else for Sarandon now. "She has no idea what it is," he said impishly. "She'll be surprised."

According to The Susan Sarandon Site, Sarandon began filming *A Whale in Montana* in April of 2003 with co-stars Donald Sutherland and Leelee Sobieski. The movie, a cross between *Ghost* and *In the Bedroom*, follows a widowed doctor who must deal with issues relating to the past, present, and future when her 7-year-old daughter's best friend starts having visions of her dead husband. The Sarandon Site also lists a number of other films Sarandon fans can look forward to if negotiations are completed successfully:

In *Rialto*, a drama set against the 1950s communist scare, Sarandon would play a mysterious woman who runs an independent movie theatre in Providence, Rhode Island. She has a tumultuous affair with a younger man, a Korean War ex-POW. When people start questioning her past and her support for artsy movies, the woman becomes the target of a communist witch-hunt.

Denial has been in development for two years. Sarandon would portray a Jewish civil rights attorney involved in a First Amendment case about a college professor who claims the Holocaust never happened.

There is talk that Sarandon has been approached to do *The Gold Coast* with Al Pacino. They would play husband and wife in this mystery/thriller based on Nelson DeMille's popular novel.

Sarandon is also in negotiations to star in a Walt Disney feature titled *Enchanted*. This film combines animation and live action to tell the story of a peasant girl in a fairy tale world who falls in love with her Prince Charming and then is banished into the New York City of the real world. Who banishes her? The Evil Queen, who Sarandon would play. The peasant girl must choose between a fairy tale happy ending and real-life love.

Donning her producer's cap, Sarandon hopes to team with Howard Koch to make *Quietus*, a western set in the 1880s. Sarandon would also star as the mother of three sons in this coming-of-age saga. Although there have been delays getting this movie underway, Sarandon indicated in an interview that she hasn't given up on this movie. Wayne Wang, who directed her in *Anywhere But Here*, would helm the film. "It's definitely a priority for me, and Wayne is still very interested," Sarandon said. "We just have to get a studio committed to the project."

Hot Flashes, a comedy reminiscent of *The First Wives Club*, would bring Sarandon, Anjelica Huston, and Sally Field together as women in the midst of menopause. These three Oscar-winners doing a rib-ald comedy together should be something to see!

In *A Class Divided*, Sarandon would star as Jane Elliot, an Iowa teacher who caused a controversy back in the 1960s by introducing an unusual lesson plan. She separated her class into two groups based on eye color and gave one group preferential treatment in order to teach students about racism. I was teaching a high school social stud-ies class at the time and remember first-hand how much fuss Elliot's experiment caused in the academic community.

There's also a possibility that Sarandon will re-team with director Robert Benton (*Twilight*) for the screen adaptation of Richard Russo's acclaimed novel *Straight Man*, a comedy about a college pro-fessor who's in the midst of a hilarious mid-life crisis. Sarandon would play the professor's love interest or wife who has issues of her own to work out. One of Sarandon's *Twilight* co-stars (Paul Newman, Gene Hackman, James Garner) may sign on for the role of the pro-fessor.

Sarandon recently signed on with Miramax to play Richard Gere's wife in the American remake of *Shall We Dance?*—my favorite Japanese movie. Jennifer Lopez is set to co-star.

In *Romance and Cigarettes*, Sarandon will appear with James Gandolfini and Kate Winslet in an all-singing, all-dancing film to be produced by Joel and Ethan Coen and directed by John Turturro. Billed as a cross between *Pennies from Heaven* and TV's *The Honeymooners*, it deals with infidelity and redemption. "Now this one should smoke!" exclaimed my journalist friend Margie Easton. (And I agree.)

That's quite a list, but personally, I'd also like to see Sarandon do a film with Morgan Freeman. And it might actually happen. During the 2002 Taos film festival, I had the honor of delivering Sarandon a second-hand message from Freeman. "Morgan Freeman wants you to call him," I said. How did I know that? During an interview with the actor, my colleague Diana Saenger asked Freeman if he planned to work with Tim Robbins again (because they were so successful together in *The Shawshank Redemption*). Freeman responded that he knew of nothing in the works with Robbins, but he wanted to do a film with Susan Sarandon and hoped she would call him. When I talked with Sarandon, she promised to make that call. It really is a small world, after all.

Is there one person Sarandon herself has been dying to play? Although mentioning Elizabeth Kubler Ross in a "Star Chat" with Bonnie Laufer of tribute.com, she added, "There are so many women that inspire me with their courage, their humor, and their frailties...there are so many stories to be told out there, so I just kind of stay open."

Clearly, despite Sarandon's political stands (and the low ratings of her *Ice Bound* TV movie), it's not any harder for her to get roles now than it was when she was younger. However, she does believe it's more difficult to find good parts—and that men are definitely paid more. She told Staci Layne Wilson of myria.com, "I'd like to make some money occasionally, but what's more important is to find roles you haven't done before. I'm not complaining. Sometimes you have to follow your heart and find things that are interesting."

CHAPTER EIGHT
A Woman of Substance

"The older I get, the more power I seem to have to help the world; I am like a snowball—the further I am rolled, the more I gain."

—Susan B. Anthony

Sarandon obviously followed her heart and brought many exciting characters to life on the big screen, but when asked about her own experiences, she declared, "My life isn't very interesting." This from a woman described in Film Encyclopedia as "one of the American screen's most dependable and versatile leading ladies." And from a woman who inspires the kind of admiration expressed by online film critic Kamal 'The Diva' Larsuel, one of the authors of *3Black Chicks Review Flicks*. Larsuel writes, "People ask me, 'If you could hang with someone, who would it be?' Well, I would like to hang out with black Hollywood (Sam Jackson, Will Smith, Vivica Fox, Jada Smith, etc.) for fun and I would love to have dinner parties with Susan Sarandon and Tim Robbins. I picture it like a roundtable meeting of the minds where you have intelligent discussions about the art of filmmaking and the plight of the world. I've marched against the Klan. Participated in the WTO. Marched with Muslim women after 9/11. There are few people I would stand on in the front line with and Susan is one of them. If I could afford it, all she

Members of the Santa Fe Boys and Girls Club
with Susan Sarandon. Photo: J. Nathan Simmons
of NewMexicoActors.com.

would have to do is call me and I'd meet her anywhere in the world and stand in solidarity."

Sarandon may not think her life is very interesting, but it's had quite an impact. She's even been approached to run for political office. "Maybe it's naiveté or cynicism," she said, "but I don't think there's a way to be effective as an elected official. The campaign reform issue is what's gone wrong. I was involved in the Green Party, but I think I'm more effective giving voice to people outside the system."

During the aftermath of the 9/11 attacks on the World Trade Center, Sarandon served food at Ground Zero, visited fire fighters, and volunteered at an emergency center. "After 9/11, I feel more of a dedicated New Yorker," she told *Variety*'s Paula Bernstein. Within the past few years, Sarandon has used her celebrity status to gain support for the following causes:

The Million Mom March. 800,000 mothers and others gathered in Washington, D.C. and in 74 communities across the United States to demand sensible gun laws. A video documents the historic Mother's Day 2000 rally—from celebrity performances to tributes to loved ones who lost their lives in gun-related violence.

The Donate-a-Phone Campaign. The goal of this campaign is to collect one million used mobile phones to benefit domestic violence victims. In a public service TV ad Susan says, "Every day, 5,000 women become victims of domestic violence. And their most powerful weapon against this atrocity may be sitting right in your own home, waiting, waiting to make a difference." Industry analysts estimate that there are currently as many as 24 million inactive mobile phones in people's homes and businesses. Once collected, the phones will either be donated to victims of domestic violence, or refurbished and sold with proceeds going to benefit domestic violence programs and organizations including the National Coalition Against Domestic Violence.

The Center for Constitutional Rights. This organization uses the law to advance human rights movements, from defending civil rights workers in the 60s to present-day struggles against police brutality, government unlawfulness and corporate complicity in human rights violations.

MADRE. Supporting women and their families in conflict zones around the world is the goal of this international human rights group, which offers medicines, counseling, and programs to seek justice.

The Raul Julia Ending Hunger Fund. Raising money for the sustainable end of hunger on the planet is the important initiative of this project.

Heifer Project International. Also aiming to end hunger, this project promotes self-reliance and builds hope by providing food-and-income producing farm animals in more than 119 countries, including rural areas of the United States.

And, of course, there's Sarandon's valuable work with UNICEF. Harry Belafonte thanked her on behalf of that international organization during his testimonial at Sarandon's Lincoln Center Gala, praising her "fierce courage, implacable intelligence, and compassion."

As a Special Representative for UNICEF, Sarandon visited Tanzania in May of 2000 in order to observe and publicize educational programs about HIV/AIDS there. She saw first-hand the toll this disease takes on children in that African nation. In December of

1999, Sarandon gave an address at UNICEF House to launch the agency's flagship publication, *The State of the World's Children 2000*. During part of her dramatic speech, she said, "When my children wake up in the morning they know they will eat breakfast, get hugs from their parents, go to a good, safe school, come home, and get help with homework. Plates are full and store windows are glittering. But at the same time the great majority of the world's children and women stand and shiver on the precipice."

In "A Day in the Life of Susan Sarandon," Sarandon wrote the following about her UNICEF trips to Tanzania and India. "We're in the cars by 7 a.m. to drive to remote villages. Local dignitaries welcome us and daub our foreheads with sandalwood and vermilion initially. I felt awkward about turning up in a village with the whole media circus and it was rather more formal than I would have liked. Going back to New York is far more surreal than anything I experience in India, because New York is such an excessively consumer culture. Some Indians may know who I am, but when I went to Tanzania, they haven't a clue. 'I'm really important,' I told them. 'I am a female basketball star.' They started laughing, realizing I was putting them on. I was very emotionally affected when I went to meet AIDS orphans. Home in New York, I went through my children's clothes, shoes and toys to send boxes to Tanzania. More than half of Tanzania does not have clean water; kids are dying just as often from dysentery as from AIDS and HIV. I promised I'd help them get wells, and I felt such a liar. A well costs $2,000. Then the guy who runs my gym suggested we raise some money, and already we've got $80,000. Some people feel celebrities have no place doing this sort of thing. But how can you live with yourself if you don't give something back?

"Late afternoon in India or Tanzania, the lack of sleep is catching up, and I'm pretty much running on empty. Mostly I don't notice because I engage with interesting people, but I go on screen when perhaps someone is talking for the umpteenth time about the importance of breastfeeding. I start to see my words coming out in bubbles.

"On the drive back, I might have a chocolate calcium chew, which I bring from New York. They're vitamins for women. I keep a bunch of power bars in my bag, and mint or rosemary scented wipes, which I have to wipe the kids' hands after a piece of pizza. I also have a mirror, a comb and a lipstick. My vanity took a knocking when I played a nun in *Dead Man Walking*, and this UNICEF work is a bit like that. When Roger, the photographer, comes and says, 'Maybe you'd just like to wipe your face,' that means I have bags under my eyes and my hair's a mess. How on earth did Audrey Hepburn, who was also a UNICEF Special Representative, travel without a hair out of place?

"Back at the hotel, I have briefings every night. I got hooked on soya milk when I had to lose all that weight for *Stepmom*. Now I find that if I'm very tired but I have a rumble in my tummy, a juice box of soya milk settles me. In bed, I write my diary. I don't aim for eloquence; I just try to remember. I might also take an over-the-counter French thing to help me sleep. I realize my job is to shine the light of celebrity on the work of the people in the field and highlight problems. You feel like an invader, but you're a very important invader.

"I'll be taken to the *baluudi* (children's) health center and perhaps to meet a mother who's an untouchable and expecting her third child, which she dreads may be a girl. In rural India they still kill girl children. One young mother had shaved her head as a pledge to the gods. Whenever you go into a home you sense a whole other scenario. Certain people look you right in the eye; you can see whether they're happy or not.

"I am blessed with great powers of empathy and imagination, which are the roots of acting and activism, only acting is much easier because you have less responsibility. I'd rather meet women as a mother than as a movie star. I hope the fact that I've been there and birthed may be a way of finding common ground. I've been so moved by how the mothers and young girls persevere under fantastic odds. Meeting these women makes me think of my own children; I miss them constantly. My kids are so healthy and cherished and so privileged, it's almost shocking.

"Sometimes I get upset by what I see, but I don't allow myself to go on that journey. The point is to keep going on and to try and get help."

Susan Sarandon strikes a pose in Taos, New Mexico
after receiving her Maverick Award. Photo: Alex Gildzen.

In a telephone conversation, I asked Sarandon to name one thing in the world she would change if she had a magic wand. She replied without skipping a beat, "I would find some way to give simple liberties to all children—a full stomach and a chance at an education and a future of dignity and hope."

During her telephone press conference for *Ice Bound*, Sarandon discussed why she and other celebrities participate in so many causes. She believes sometimes it's the only way worthwhile causes can get media attention. Regarding a New York protest over the cutting of funds for AIDS patients, Sarandon said TV cameras were sent to cover the demonstration when they knew she and Rosie Perez would appear. Sarandon pointed out that if the main speaker at various events is an actor, there's more interest. "A lot of the time it's just really an attempt to give people access to information," she stated. "It's never trying to tell people what to think. But I think they should know."

Meanwhile back in the show-biz world, film critics and movie fans alike continue to rave about Sarandon. Phil Hall, contributing editor for the online *Film Threat*, writes, "She looks a damn lot sexier than any of the young actresses littering up the screen today."

Nathaniel Rogers of Film Experience.com extols Sarandon's virtues on an Internet shrine he's set up for her. Naming her one of the top twenty actors of the 90s, Rogers explains, "She makes aging seem ridiculously sexy. She's like a fine wine. She subverted typecasting and went from a hot-blooded red-hot actress to celebrity earth mother and didn't loose her sensuality in the process. It's all about longevity—Sarandon has outlasted them all."

And Chris Baker, who maintains the unofficial Susan Sarandon Site, claims he chose Sarandon because "She's the real deal, a proper actress, sharp, sassy, and seriously sexy." Fueled by many frustrating hours spent trawling the internet for information about his favorite actress, Baker decided to start The Susan Sarandon Site in mid-1998. "The site started out back in 1998 with a two-page filmography and has since grown into a 50+ page monster which attracts up to 2,000 visitors a day," writes Baker. When not working on updates for the site, Baker is a film extra who has worked on such films as *Wit, Johnny English, Highlander: Endgame,* and *Killing Me Softly.*

Contributing regularly to Baker's Sarandon site, freelance film critic Mack Bates credits *Thelma & Louise* with influencing his desire to become a filmmaker in his own right. In keeping with that goal, he picked Film Studies as his major at the University of Wisconsin.

As of July 7, 2002, Sarandon's films have grossed over 850 million dollars, according to *The Movie Times*. The average gross of her last ten movies through that date was close to 40 million dollars. She has one movie that made over 100 million dollars and is still going strong. Which one? *The Rocky Horror Picture Show*, of course. (Never underestimate the power of those midnight flicks.)

In celebration of Sarandon's Maverick Award, the 2002 Taos Talking Picture Festival program booklet offered the following provocative summary of her extraordinary influence:

Fearless, impassioned, outspoken—she is a familiar voice for human rights—Sarandon could be considered an unintentional role model for a society terrified by aging. She's also an actor who has proven that Hollywood movies can matter. Those two qualities in themselves make Susan Sarandon every bit as heroic as her characters. By reaching deep within herself each time out to reveal an essential truth, she has earned the right to reign for more than Hollywood's standard term of office.

No doubt about it, a surprising journey awaited little Susan Abigail Tomalin, who was born to Phillip and Lenora Tomalin on October 4, 1946, in Jackson Heights, New York. Watching her grow up in Edison, New Jersey, with eight younger siblings, could anyone have foreseen the dramatic accomplishments of this "introverted and spacey student" (her own words) who sometimes challenged the nuns about religious doctrines and who, as a teenager, was arrested for participating in Vietnam and Civil Rights protests?

In January of 2000, Sarandon visited with a small group of Columbia University students about to embark on their own journeys. Giving them the kind of advice only a true maverick would offer, she encouraged each student to take a chance and be open to possibilities—no matter what others might think. "Prepare to be surprised," she said.

For Susan Sarandon, I suspect arrival is not the reward—it's the journey that counts.

"Susan can do and give you anything you want in front of a camera and be incredibly effective."

—Burr Steers, director/writer, *Igby Goes Down*

ANNOTATED FILMOGRAPHY

"It's a slender curtain between theater and life."

—Susan Sarandon as Celimene in *Illuminata*

During a career spanning over thirty years, Susan Sarandon has brought many unforgettable characters to life on screen. She's made us laugh, cry, think, wonder—and understand ourselves a little better after watching her passionate performances. Before our very eyes, she went from hippie daughter to grieving mother. In between, she played such diverse characters as a flamboyant actress, a sexy baseball groupie, a dictator's mistress, a disillusioned waitress, a vampire's victim, and a dedicated nun. Here are brief descriptions of Sarandon's movies from 1970 – 2003.

1970 – *Joe*. John Avildsen directed this violent film about a bigot, played by Peter Boyle, who meets a wealthy businessman and learns his chilling secret. As Melissa Compton, the businessman's hippie daughter, Susan Sarandon made an impressive movie debut and revealed much more than her acting talent.

1971 – *The Apprentice*. This film explored the problems of being a French Canadian. Sarandon, again displaying her considerable physical beauty, portrayed Elizabeth Hawkins, an English

Canadian involved in a relationship with a young French Canadian man.

1971 – *Lady Liberty*. Sophia Loren and William Devane co-starred in this romantic comedy about an Italian woman who tries to bring a special cheese into the United States. Sarandon had a small part as an attractive young lady named Sally.

1974 – *Lovin' Molly*. Sarandon played the supporting role of Sarah in this drama about two friends in love with the same woman. Although directed by Sidney Lumet and starring Anthony Perkins, Beau Bridges, and Blythe Danner, this movie version of Larry McMurtry's *Leaving Cheyenne* achieved little success with critics or at the box office. Notable only for Sarandon because it gave her the opportunity to learn more about acting from the director and stars.

1974 – *The Front Page*. Billy Wilder's film version of this classic stage comedy presented another chance for Sarandon to learn from a respected director and from established actors. She played Peggy Grant, the woman engaged to Jack Lemmon's character— a reporter who wants to quit and do something else. Walter Matthau portrayed an editor who will do anything to stop him. *The Front Page* earned a Golden Globe nomination in the Best Musical or Comedy category, but it lost out to *The Longest Yard*.

1974 – *June Moon* (TV). Sarandon plays a vixen who lures a naïve songwriter in this satire of Tin Pan Alley circa 1929. Based on the play by Ring Lardner and George S. Kaufman, the television film lost something in transition—despite appearances by Jack Cassidy, Estelle Parsons, and Stephen Sondheim as the wise-cracking, piano-playing narrator.

1974 – *F. Scott Fitzgerald and the Last of the Belles* (TV). Written by James Costigan and directed by George Schaefer, this television drama featured Richard Chamberlain as the famous writer and Blythe Danner as wife Zelda, a woman obsessed with becoming a ballerina. Sarandon portrayed Ailie Calhoun, a southern belle in one of Fitzgerald's stories that took place during World War I.

1975 – *The Great Waldo Pepper*. As ill-fated Mary Beth to Robert Redford's glory-seeking Waldo, Sarandon joined a flying circus and walked on the wing of an airplane in George Roy Hill's salute to the early days of aviation. Redford and Sarandon? Now there's a pairing I'd like to see on the big screen again.

1975 – *The Rocky Horror Picture Show*. "Touch-a touch-a touch-a touch me," sang Sarandon in this transsexual musical about a straight-laced couple (with Barry Bostwick) finding their moral world turned upside down after being trapped in Frank-N-Furter's (Tim Curry) weird castle. (It's not surprising Sarandon can carry a tune. She inherited that talent from her father, Phillip Tomalin, who was once a Big Band singer.) Outrageous costumes and songs like the "Time Warp" added to the *Rocky Horror* fun. Surprisingly, appearing in this campy flick failed to damage Sarandon's career. Instead, it demonstrated her versatility. Online film critic A. J. Hakari remarks about the movie's cult status in his 2002 review. "Twenty-seven years after its debut in theatres, this bizarre musical is still making a killing at midnight screenings across the country," he writes. Sarandon says much the same thing in her comments on the 25th Anniversary Edition DVD. "*Rocky Horror* has probably kept a lot of art house theaters in business over the years because of revenue for midnight screenings—even if showings at regular hours flop," she observes.

1976 – *The Great Smokey Roadblock*. Sarandon played Ginny, a prostitute (with a heart of gold, of course), in John Leone's comedy/drama starring Henry Fonda as a trucker about to lose his rig. Serving also as co-producer, she put in many extra hours working behind the scenes.

1976 – *Dragonfly*. Portraying Chloe, a woman who becomes romantically involved with a man (Beau Bridges) released from a mental institution and trying to track down his family, Sarandon was cast here in a typical 70s love-interest role. Directed by Gilbert

Cates, this little-seen drama failed to showcase Sarandon's developing acting range.

1977 – *Checkered Flag or Crash*. Sarandon tried her hand at action adventure in this B-movie about a jungle road race. She played C. C. Wainwright to Larry Hagman's Bo Cochran, an off-road racing promoter. Is it true Sarandon bought up all the prints of this one? Not really, but she probably should have.

1977 – *The Other Side of Midnight*. Playing Catherine Alexander Douglas, a spurned alcoholic wife in this glossy film version of Sidney Sheldon's bestseller, Sarandon proved she could age on screen from 17 to 35. She also brought depth and humor to a soap-operaish character who experienced many changes during the course of the film. According to critic Pauline Kael, Sarandon "provided the sprightliest moments in *The Other Side of Midnight*."

1978 – *Pretty Baby*. In her first film for French director Louis Malle, Sarandon was cast as Hattie, a New Orleans prostitute with a beautiful 12-year-old daughter whose virginity is auctioned off to a photographer. Kael described some of Sarandon's nude scenes as "mysteriously beautiful"—but the most scandalous nudity here belonged to then pre-teen Brooke Shields, who portrayed the daughter.

1978 – *King of the Gypsies*. Sarandon seemed too young to play Rose, the mother of a young man (Eric Roberts) chosen by his grandfather (Sterling Hayden) to be the next King of the Gypsies. Still, she worked hard to make Rose memorable amid a strong ensemble cast that also included a formidable Shelley Winters and the always-watchable Annie Potts.

1979 – *Something Short of Paradise*. Sarandon played Madeline Ross in this little romantic comedy about two New Yorkers who try to find happiness despite various obstacles. David Steinberg co-starred. The film's title says it all.

1980 – **Atlantic City**. Sarandon was Sally, a wannabe croupier with a philandering husband, to Burt Lancaster's Lou, an old-time hood, in Louis Malle's extraordinary movie about the old giving way to the new. Sarandon's sexy "washing with lemons" scene remains a classic. *Premiere Magazine* (March, 2003) listed it as #54 in "The 100 Greatest Movie Moments of All Time." Sarandon reports, "People still send me lemons." Both she and Lancaster earned Oscar nominations (Sarandon's first and Lancaster's last) for their poignant performances here, but they lost out to *On Golden Pond*'s Katharine Hepburn and Henry Fonda.

1980 – **Loving Couples**. Sarandon played Stephanie, one member of the two "loving couples," in this comedy about spouse swapping. Shirley MacLaine, James Coburn, and Stephen Elliott portrayed the others involved. Just an average flick, but it helped Sarandon sharpen her comedic skills.

1982 – **Who Am I This Time?** (TV). In this television film based on one of Kurt Vonnegut's short stories, Sarandon co-starred with Christopher Walken as a telephone operator who auditions for a part in a local amateur production of *A Streetcar Named Desire*. She falls in with Walken, a shy man who becomes the characters he plays on stage. According to Doug Pratt's Laserdisc Review, Sarandon "embodies her part so accurately and seductively that while you are watching her nothing else matters."

1982 – **Tempest**. As the free-spirited Aretha, Sarandon joined John Cassavetes, Gena Rowlands, Raul Julia, and Molly Ringwald in Paul Mazursky's update of William Shakespeare's play. She radiated sensuality again in a performance combining light sarcasm, warmth, and sexiness. Critic Ron Small wrote, "Sarandon is a comely vision, impeccably tan, with short, amber, curled hair. She radiates more pure carnality in *Tempest* than she has since...*Atlantic City*." No wonder assistant director Franco Amurri fell for Sarandon during the filming of this romantic comedy.

1983 – **The Hunger**. A daring love scene between Sarandon and Cathrine Deneuve emerged as the highlight of this stylish vampire-themed flick. Sarandon portrayed Dr. Sarah Roberts, a researcher of premature aging, who falls prey to the bisexual female vampire Miriam Blaylock (Deneuve). David Bowie also co-starred, and Tony Scott directed.

1984 – *The Buddy System*. This little romantic drama failed to do much for Sarandon's movie career, but it offered her an opportunity to work with friend Richard Dreyfuss. Sarandon played Emily, an insecure single mother whose son tries to bring her and his truant officer together. Where have we heard that one before?

1985 – *A.D. Anno Domini* (TV). Sarandon played Livilla in this miniseries chronicling the life of Jesus's disciples after his death. Other big names in the cast included Anthony Andrews, Colleen Dewhurst, Ava Gardner, and James Mason.

1985 – *Mussolini: The Decline and Fall of Il Duce* (TV). Sarandon joined Bob Hoskins and Anthony Hopkins in this television movie about events in Italy during World War II. She portrayed Edda Ciano to Hoskins's Mussolini. Hopkins played Mussolini's son who tries to get the dictator to break with Hitler.

1985 – *Compromising Positions*. In this comic mystery based on Susan Isaac's novel, Sarandon played Judith Singer, a bored suburban housewife turned amateur sleuth. Raul Julia, portraying a detective trying to solve the murder of a philandering dentist, has many suspects in the case, including Sarandon's character. Unfortunately, here's a film that underwhelmed moviegoers and critics alike.

1986 – *Women of Valor* (TV). Sarandon played Colonel Margaret Jessup in this television drama about U. S. Army nurses who were captured and impressed by the Japanese troops in the Philippines during World War II. Sarandon's character assumed a protective attitude toward a younger nurse (Kristy McNichol). *Women of Valor* won an award from the American Cinema Editors as Best Edited TV Special.

1987 – *The Witches of Eastwick*. Back in top form in this outrageous movie version of John Updike's bestseller, Sarandon scorched the screen as Jane Spofford, a lonely woman who changes from dull wallflower to seductive siren after consorting with the devil himself, played flamboyantly by Jack Nicholson. Cher (who landed the role Sarandon originally thought she was going to play) and Michelle Pfeiffer portrayed her friends who also discover supernatural powers. Sarandon's fiery cello-playing sequence became almost as famous as her *Atlantic City* lemons.

1988 – *Sweet Hearts Dance*. Sarandon played long-suffering Sandra Boon to Don Johnson's Wiley Boon in this uneven drama about a married couple splitting up after many years of wedded life. An emphasis on the friendship between Johnson's character and his buddy, played by Jeff Daniels, a man just entering into a new romantic relationship, took the spotlight away from Sarandon's performance.

1988 – *Bull Durham*. As the sexy, uninhibited Annie Savoy in this comedy/drama about America's favorite pastime, Sarandon found one of her best roles, one that should have earned her another Oscar nomination. Co-stars Kevin Costner and Tim Robbins played baseball players involved with Sarandon's aging groupie ("I believe in the Church of Baseball"), but she stole the show. Paul Lewis, of EFilmCritic.com, wrote, "Susan Sarandon sizzles as Savoy in one of the plain sexiest, smartest screen siren roles of the last twenty years." Filmmaker Ron Shelton credits Sarandon for putting him at ease in his directorial debut here. And, as we all know, she did even more for Robbins.

1989 – *The January Man*. In this Pat O'Connor-directed thriller about catching a serial killer, Sarandon played Christine Starkey, a rather subdued and moody romantic who Kevin Kline's character once loved. He's a disgraced cop called back to solve the crime, and she's now his sister-in-law. Although generally panned by critics, I found it quite suspenseful and entertaining.

1989 – *A Dry White Season*. Sarandon played Melanie Bruwer, a journalist ally of a South African teacher, portrayed by Donald Sutherland, who began to realize the evils of apartheid and then fought against them. The great Marlon Brando also appeared in this movie, an enlightening film with a strong social conscience—one Sarandon couldn't pass up despite her limited time on camera.

1990 – *White Palace*. In this unusual romantic movie, Sarandon played Nora Baker, a woman much older than her lover (James Spader) who acts ashamed of her job as a waitress and of her age. Sarandon pulled out all the stops here. She's sex personified in a refreshingly different version of May/December relationships. What, no Oscar nomination? Sometimes there's no justice in the world.

1991 – *Thelma & Louise*. Critic Rita Kempley of the *Washington Post* described Sarandon's Louise Sawyer as "fiercely hard-boiled," whereas Peter Travers of *Rolling Stone* wrote that Sarandon's performance was "stunningly poignant." It garnered her another Oscar nomination for Best Actress. Geena Davis (also nominated) and Sarandon made a striking odd couple rebelling against the men in their lives, and both are unforgettable in this landmark female buddy movie, expertly directed by Ridley Scott. Screenwriter Callie Khouri won the Best Original Screenplay Oscar for her groundbreaking work here.

1991 – *Light Sleeper*. Sarandon playing an upscale drug dealer? Yes, and she received great critical notices for her *Light Sleeper* role as Ann, a woman who decides to sell cosmetics instead of drugs. "Commanding," "intelligent," "delightful" are among adjectives used to describe Sarandon's Ann. Willem Dafoe co-stars as one of her employees who does some soul-searching of his own in this compelling Paul Schrader drama.

1991 – *The Player.* Sarandon had a cameo as herself in this clever Robert Altman satire of Hollywood. While working on the film, she met Julia Roberts, who later became one of her best friends.

1992 – **Lorenzo's Oil**. Another Oscar nomination came Sarandon's way for her passionate portrayal of Irish-American linguist Michaela Odone, a mother helping her Italian banker husband, played by Nick Nolte, find a cure for their desperately ill son in this film version of a true story. Directed by George Miller, who is also an MD, the movie exuded realism while depicting parental love carried to the max.

1992 – **Bob Roberts**. Taking a small role in Tim Robbins' mockumentary about a folk-singing, manipulative, conservative politician, Sarandon played Tawna Titan, one of the television news commentators who chronicled the man's rise to fame.

1994 – **Little Women**. Sarandon played Marmie March, the wise and caring mother of four daughters, in this film version of Louisa May Alcott's classic post-Civil War novel. Her strong performance was one of the movie's highlights. Sarandon's "Marmie" came across as a model mom, the kind any daughter would be fortunate to have now as well as back in the 1860s. Internet critic Terry Brogan said, "Sarandon is probably the only woman who could take on the role of Marmie and still emerge with a sense of professional dignity, not to mention career, intact. In the book her character is so insufferably stoic and noble, you sometimes want to shake her hard and tell her to wake up to the realities of the war. But through...Sarandon's interpretation, the character is now more tempered and convincing as a struggling single parent who seeks to instill basic common decency in her children." Australian Gillian Armstrong directed the movie masterfully, and Winona Ryder, Trini Alvarado, Samantha Mathis, Claire Danes, and Kirsten Dunst also gave praiseworthy performances here.

1994 – **Safe Passage**. In his review of *Safe Passage*, Roger Ebert called Sarandon "invaluable." He wrote that she "just continues to grow as an actress and inhabits her characters as naturally as favorite old sweaters." Sarandon played Mag Singer, an unhappy wife and mother who has a premonition about one of her seven sons, a young man serving his country overseas. Sam Shepard co-starred

as the sometimes-blind father in this drama about family problems and dynamics.

1994 – **The Client**. Sarandon played Reggie Love, an outspoken
attorney hired by a youngster in this movie version of John
Grisham's popular novel. Her one-upmanship scenes with
Tommy Lee Jones, who portrayed the hard-nosed district attorney, were so convincing I thought they meant every barb they
flung at each other. The result? Another well-deserved Oscar
nomination.

1995 – **Dead Man Walking**. As Sister Helen Prejean, a nun counseling a death-row inmate played by Sean Penn, Sarandon finally
won an Oscar. Tim Robbins directed this provocative cinematic
exploration of the death penalty. Sarandon's powerful performance emerged as one of her best ever. Critic Kevin Laforest, who
believes Sarandon's acting is "always wonderfully right and
human," called her turn as Sister Prejean "touching and believable" in his review for the *Montreal Film Journal*.

1996 – **James and the Giant Peach**. Sarandon voiced the role of a
French-accented Spider in this film treatment of Roald Dahl's
well-known children's book. Using a creative combination of
live-action and stop-motion animation, director Henry Selick created a wondrous cinematic fantasy about a young boy's trip from
England to New York inside a huge peach.

1998 – **Twilight**. Paul Newman, Gene Hackman, and James Garner
joined Sarandon in director Robert Benton's murder mystery, a
contemporary flick with old-fashioned film noir undertones.
Sarandon played glamorous movie star Catherine Ames, who
may or may not be implicated in the death of her first husband.
"*Twilight's* dead-on cast makes even the most familiar twists and
turns riveting and entertaining," wrote Joshua Klein in his review
for *The Onion*.

1998 – **Illuminata**. Sarandon played Celimene, another aging
actress, in John Turturro's artsy film about a turn-of-the-century
theater company. Sarandon's flamboyant send-up of self-

involved celebrities is a comic gem, especially in her seduction scene with Turturro, the film's protagonist (a new playwright). That sequence gave the term "casting couch" a whole new twist.

1998 – *Stepmom*. Critic Kenneth Turan wrote, "Susan Sarandon and Julia Roberts seem to have great fun sparring with each other [in *Stepmom*]." Right! These two real-life friends enjoyed working together (as co-producers as well as co-stars) on this tearjerker directed by Chris Columbus. As Jackie Harrison, Sarandon brilliantly conveyed the hostility of an ex-wife who loses her husband (Ed Harris) and children to a younger woman (Roberts). When faced with a serious illness, Sarandon's character softens and makes peace with her rival for the good of the entire family. The San Diego Film Critics Society voted Sarandon Best Actress of the Year for her heartbreaking performance. Lots of Kleenex needed while watching this one!

1999 – *Cradle Will Rock*. Sarandon played Italian fascist Margherita Sarfatti in this sweeping film about politics, art, and censorship in the USA during the 1930s. Her character, Mussolini's former mistress, sells art masterpieces to American industrialists in order to help Il Duce's war machine. Ian Waldron-Mantgani, the UK Critic, wrote that *Cradle* came out "without finding what it was looking for," but he admitted the film had many qualities that make us want to like it—it's "ambitious, left-wing, and rich in photography, with a great cast, flamboyant characters, and an interesting setting." Filled with depictions of real-life people from Depression Era history, *Cradle* was directed by Tim Robbins and featured Angus Macfayden as Orson Welles, John Cusack as Nelson Rockefeller, Ruben Bladés as Diego Rivera, and Cary Elwes as John Houseman. Sarandon had very little time on camera, but she made every moment count. "I was primed to play a character that gets to wear killer clothes and have great hair and makeup and wear pumps," Sarandon told Mack Bates in his award-winning interview.

1999 – ***Anywhere But Here***. In direct contrast to her "Marmie March" role in *Little Women*, Sarandon took on the role of Adele August, the quirky mother of a more practical daughter played by Natalie Portman. "After playing a nun and all these moms, the other kind of moms," Sarandon explained in her interview with Mack Bates, " it was tempting to do somebody different, which this character is because she was completely over the top—someone who didn't take her eyeliner off and wore these outrageous clothes." In the film's press notes, Sarandon described Adele as a mother who loves her daughter, but is "misguided and self-serving." While projecting excitement and a sense of power in this mostly unsympathetic role, Sarandon also displayed her unique comic flair. The chemistry between Sarandon and Portman worked wonders here, as did Wayne Wang's sensitive direction.

1999 – ***Our Friend Martin***. Combining cartoon animation and historical footage, this elementary school video aimed to teach kids about the life of Martin Luther King, Jr. Sarandon voiced one of the characters (Mrs. Clark). Whoopi Goldberg, Danny Glover, LeVar Burton, Ashley Judd, Samuel L. Jackson, Ed Asner, and James Earl Jones also lent their voices to this important educational project.

1999 – ***Earthly Possessions*** (TV). Sarandon as a dowdy housewife? Puh-leez. Scott Tobias of *The Onion A.V. Club* writes, "She's uniquely unsuited to play it," and complains that she is forced "to obscure her vibrant sensuality and intelligence." Still, after Sarandon's character is taken hostage by kidnapper Stephen Dorff, she develops interesting chemistry with him—and things liven up. James Lapine directed this television movie based on the novel by Anne Tyler.

2000 – ***Joe Gould's Secret***. Sarandon appeared here in a cameo as painter Alice Neel, one of the people supporting the eccentric Joe Gould (Ian Holm), a homeless man supposedly writing a comprehensive "Oral History of the World." Stanley Tucci directed and starred as Joe Mitchell, a writer for *The New Yorker* back in the 1930s and 40s. Sarandon took this small role because she wanted to work with Tucci and Holm. Now it's one of her favorite New York movies "because it transports one back into the time when the Village was a village, and artists knew and supported each other."

2000 – ***Rugrats in Paris: The Movie***. Sarandon won the Kids' Choice Award as favorite voice in an animated movie for her amusing vocal inflections as Coco La Bouche, the evil businesswoman who hates kids, in this Rugrats family flick. Eat your heart out, Cruella deVil.

2001 – ***Cats & Dogs***. Adopting a more soothing tone, Sarandon voiced the role of Ivy, a compassionate alley dog who watches out after a young Beagle pup (Tobey Maguire's voice) in this live-action comedy about the hairy war between cats and dogs.

2002 – ***The Banger Sisters***. Although Sarandon played a more challenging role than co-star Goldie Hawn in this comedy about the reunion of two aging rock groupies, both talented actresses did their best with the film's frivolous script. When these former pals get together after 20 years apart, everything changes for each of them. Unfortunately, their reunion is sometimes more painful than funny to watch. Sarandon excelled as Lavinia, an uptight woman married to a wealthy lawyer, who doesn't want anyone to know about her past. But after old friend Suzette (Hawn) comes back into her life, Lavinia begins to realize how much joy she is missing. Eva Amurri, Sarandon's real-life daughter who plays her on-screen daughter here, evoked the most laughs from me with her hilarious spoiled-brat antics. "Fresh and funny, this charming, bittersweet film makes the most of the considerable comic talents of Goldie Hawn and Susan Sarandon," says MaryAnn Johanson, of FlickFilosopher.com, in her glowing review. Okay, I know the film's message is "be true to yourself." But why emphasize it by glorifying promiscuity? Watching gifted actresses like Hawn and Sarandon lower themselves to such material put me in a deep funk.

2002 – *Igby Goes Down*. As Mimi, a rich woman with an incorrigible son, Sarandon shared some choice scenes with Kieran Culkin (who played Igby) in this dark comedy written and directed by Burr Steers. Author Gore Vidal, Steers's uncle and godfather to one of Sarandon's sons, appears briefly as a headmaster of one of the numerous schools Igby gets kicked out of. Critic Susan Granger called the movie scathing and incredibly funny. "Steers continually surprises and delights with his quirky characters, sharp insights, and saucy dialogue," she wrote. Sarandon's flashy performance as Mimi earned the actress a Golden Globe "Best Supporting Actress" nomination.

2002 – *Moonlight Mile*. Sarandon portrayed Jo-Jo, a mother grieving over the loss of her daughter as the result of a random act of violence, in Brad Silberling's haunting film inspired by a similar loss of his own. Excruciating realism peppered with unexpected humor helped make this movie something special. Online critic Jill Cozzi (who listed *Moonlight Mile* as one of the 15 best movies of 2002 on her MixedReviews.com web site) writes that the film is "held together by letter-perfect performances by Susan Sarandon and Dustin Hoffman as parents coping in vastly different ways, Jake Gyllenhaal as the girl's guilt-ridden fiancé, and a breakthrough performance by newcomer Ellen Pompeo as a young woman similarly damaged by death." The movie's uplifting message? According to critic Jeffrey Chen (of windowtothemovies.com), the lesson proves to be one that common sense has helped many to realize—learn to let go.

2003 – *Frank Herbert's Children of the Dune* (TV). Based on the second and third books of Herbert's series of sci-fi novels, this miniseries featured Sarandon as the wicked Princess Wensicia, a manipulative woman who proves the old saying, "Power corrupts and absolute power corrupts absolutely." Sarandon's wild hairdos almost overshadowed her splendid interpretation of the villainous princess.

2003 – *Ice Bound* (TV). In this fact-based television drama directed by Roger Spottiswoode, Sarandon portrayed Dr. Jerri Nielsen, a doctor stationed at the South Pole who discovers she has breast cancer. Sarandon excelled at showing the woman's changing attitude about her assignment and her colleagues. The film's icy climate contrasted with its heartwarming message: help sometimes comes from unexpected sources. Although TV columnist Bill Mann found a few drawbacks in *Ice Bound*, he called the movie "a gripping tale of survival" and "an intelligent film about people cooperating." Regarding Sarandon's performance, Mann concluded, "This performance leaves little doubt about her impressive acting talent."

"Susan Sarandon has a kind of inner force. People listen to her."

—Augusto Odone, portrayed by Nick Nolte in *Lorenzo's Oil*

BIBLIOGRAPHY

"The trouble with facts is that there are so many of them."

—Samuel McChord Crothers, *The Gentle Reader*

While searching for information about Susan Sarandon, I found the following books, articles and websites quite enlightening and very helpful. Of course, I'm sure there are many more sources available. However, in the writing game, there's always a deadline.

BOOKS:

An Actor Prepares. Constantin Stanislavsky (Routledge, 1948). The great Russian drama teacher/director described his new (for that period) style of acting in this landmark book—which some refer to as "the actor's Bible." Many of Sarandon's performances illustrate the effectiveness of applying Stanislavsky's advice.

Dead Man Walking: The Shooting Script. Tim Robbins, Helen Prejean (Newmarket Press, 1997). This script for the movie that earned Sarandon a Best Actress Oscar also includes footnotes detailing why some scenes worked and others had to be cut.

Fifty Celebrate Fifty. Editors of *More Magazine* (Meredith Books, 2002). Susan Sarandon wrote the foreword to this compilation of inspiring tales about women who see midlife as an opportunity for growth.

For Keeps. Pauline Kael (Dutton—Penguin Books, 1994). Over 275 film reviews by one of America's most distinguished movie critics are included in this huge, impressive book. Among the Sarandon films reviewed are *Atlantic City*, *Pretty Baby*, and *The Other Side of Midnight*.

Great Women of Film. Helene Lumme and Mika Manninen (Watson-Guptill Publications, 2002). Sarandon appears in this enlightening book as one of thirty fascinating women who have achieved success in the world of film—some behind the camera, others by acting.

Nader: Crusader, Spoiler, Icon. Justin Martin (Perseus Publishing, 2002). A revealing investigative biography of Ralph Nader— which should interest Sarandon fans because of her support for Nader's presidential campaign on the Green Party ticket in 2000.

Ridley Scott: Close Up. Paul Sammon (Thunder's Mouth Press, 1999). One of the films discussed here by director Ridley Scott is *Thelma & Louise.* He explains his admiration for Sarandon's acting talent and the reasons he wanted her to play "Louise."

Screen Acting. Alan Lovell and Peter Kramer, editors (Routledge, 2000). Susan Sarandon is included among the stars whose acting styles are discussed in this exploration of the relationship between script and performance. Lovell's chapter 7 ("In Praise of Older Women") is devoted entirely to Sarandon.

Susan Sarandon: Actress–Activist. Marc Shapiro (Prometheus Books, 2001). This unauthorized biography of Sarandon covers her life up to 2001. It includes excellent background information about Sarandon's personal life as well as her career.

ARTICLES:

"The 100 Greatest Movie Moments." Glenn Kenny (head writer), *Premiere*, March 2003.

"Activist Leanings." Paula Bernstein, *Variety*, October 20, 2002.

"The Anti Star." Robert Hofler, *Buzz*, February 1995.

"Apple Pie, Motherhood and Sex." Robin Abcarian, *Los Angeles Times*, October 24, 1999.

"*Atlantic City.*" Review by Betty Jo Tucker, ReelTalk Movie Reviews, reeltalkreviews.com.

"*Anywhere But Here.*" Review by Betty Jo Tucker, ReelTalk Movie Reviews.

"Brad Silberling on *Moonlight Mile.*" Betty Jo Tucker, ReelTalk Movie Reviews.

"*The Banger Sisters.*" Review by MaryAnn Johanson, FlickFilosopher.com.

"*Bull Durham.*" Review by John Larsen, Lightviews.com.

"*Bull Durham.*" Review by Paul Lewis, eFilmCritic.com

"*The Client.*" Review by Joan Ellis, joanellis.com.

"*Compromising Positions.*" Review by Roger Ebert, *Chicago Sun-Times*, August 30, 1985.

"A Conversation with Erika Christensen and Eva Amurri." Bonnie Laufer, *Tribute* Star Chat.

"*Cradle Will Rock.*" Review by Gabriel Shanks, Mixed Reviews.net.

"*Cradle Will Rock.*" Review by Ian Waldron-Mantgani, UKCritic.com.

"*Dead Man Walking.*" Review by Kathleen Carroll, *Film Scouts*.

"*Dead Man Walking.*" Review by Kevin Laforest, *Montreal Film Journal.*

"Down Wrong Roads (*Igby Goes Down*)." Diana Saenger, ReelTalk Movie Reviews, September 2002.

"Hollywood Couple Face Critics after Mauling on Fringe." Tom Peterkin, news.telegraph.co.uk, August 18, 2002.

"*Illuminata*." Review by Susan Granger, SSG Syndicate, SusanGranger.com.

"*Ice Bound*: A Gripping Tale of Survival." Bill Mann, Northbay.com, April 20, 2003.

"Jake Gyllenhaal: Shooting for the Stars." Jenny Peters, *Upfront* Online, 2002.

"*Joe*." Review by Ryan Cracknell, ReelTalk Movie Reviews.

"*Light Sleeper*." Review by Walter Chaw, ReelTalk Movie Reviews, June 2003.

"Like the Mona Lisa." Betty Jo Tucker, ReelTalk Movie Reviews, December 2002.

"*Little Women*." Review by Terry Brogan, Safe.

"*Lorenzo's Oil*." Review by Chris Hicks, *Deseret News*.

"Lorenzo's Trial." Lucy Atkins, *The Guardian*, October 15, 2002.

"Loving Susan." Taos Talking Picture Festival 2002 Program Book.

"Making a Sweet Margherita." Annlee Ellingson, Boxoffice Online (cover story).

"A Memorable Film Festival." Betty Jo Tucker, *Colorado Senior Beacon*, September 2002.

"Michael Caine Still Driven To Succeed." Bruce Kirkland. *Toronto Sun*, February 2, 2003.

"Modern Romance Fails to Heat Up the Screen." Diana Saenger, *Script*, November/December 1997.

"*Moonlight Mile*." Review by Jill Cozzi, MixedReviews.net, 2002.

"*Moonlight Mile*." Review by Kevin Laforest, *Montreal Film Journal*.

"*Moonlight Mile.*" Review by Patty Miller-Marshall, *The Popcorn Chronicles*.

"Mother's Pride: Sarandon's Daughter Follows in Her Acting Footsteps." Andrew Dougan, Online *Evening Times*, February 4, 2003.

"Ms. Sarandon: A Triple Threat." Paul Fischer, *Film Monthly*, September 18, 2002.

"*The Nazi Officer's Wife.*" Review by Donald J. Levit, ReelTalk Movie Reviews, 2003.

"No Biz Like Show Biz for Barry Bostwick." Betty Jo Tucker, ReelTalk Movie Reviews.

"Not So Suddenly Susan." Dennis Hamill, *New York Daily News*, November 7, 1999.

"*Pretty Baby.*" Review by Frank Wilkins, ReelTalk Movie Reviews, 2003.

"The Prime of Susan Sarandon." Ben Yagoda, *American Film*, May 1991.

"*The Rocky Horror Picture Show.*" Review by A. J. Hakari, The Snack Bar, www.ajhakari.com.

"*The Rocky Horror Picture Show.*" Review by Joshua Vasquez, ReelTalk Movie Reviews, 2003.

"*Safe Passage.*" Review by Roger Ebert, *Chicago Sun Times*.

"*Safe Passage.*" Review by Joan Ellis, An Illusion Review, www.joanellis.com.

"Sarandon, Seriously." Aimee Lee Ball, *Mother Jones*, February-March 1989.

"Sarandon's Roots are GOP." Scott Maxwell, *Orlando Sentinel*, March 25, 2003.

"Simply the Best: Susan Sarandon." Mack Bates, *The Leader*, December 6, 1999.

"Smart, Sassy, Sultry Sarandon." Braden Phillips, *Variety*, August 28, 2000.

"Speaking Out Makes Sense to Sarandon." Robert L. Laurence, *San Diego Union-Tribune*, April 18, 2003.

"Star's Conscience Shines." Mari Florence, *Variety*, March 10, 1998.

"*Stepmom.*" Review by Susan Granger, SSG Syndicate, Susan Granger.com.

"*Stepmom.*" Review by Kenneth Turan, *Los Angeles Times*.

"Suddenly Susan." Staci Layne Wilson, Myria.com.

"Susan Sarandon Breaks the Rule That Says Actresses Can't Age." Karen Durbin, *The New York Times*, September 8, 2002.

"Susan Sarandon Gala." Betty Jo Tucker, ReelTalk Movie Reviews, May 2003.

"Susan Sarandon Interview." Sheryl Altman, Women.com.

"Susan Sarandon Interviewed by Adrian Wootton," *The Guardian*, November 12, 1999.

"Susan Sarandon Interviewed by Gavin Smith," *Film Comment Magazine*, Film Society of Lincoln Center, 2003.

"Susan Sarandon: No Longer the Ingenue!" Barney Cohen, *Cosmopolitan*, January 1984.

"*Tempest.*" Review by Ron Small, Ron's Movie Reviews.

"*Thelma & Louise.*" Review by Chris Baker, The Susan Sarandon Site.

"*Thelma & Louise.*" Review by Peter Travers, *Rolling Stone*.

"*Thelma & Louise.*" Review by Rita Kempley, *The Washington Post*, May 24, 1991.

"Those Fabulous Adams Sisters." Betty Jo Tucker, ReelTalk Movie Reviews.

"Tim Robbins: Why I'll Always Be a Misfit." Sunday Magazine, *Herald Sun*, April 30, 2000.

"Traitors: Loud Mouth Celebs 'Side with Saddam' When They Criticize Pres. Bush's Iraq War Plan." Art Dworken, *National Examiner*, February 2003.

"*Twilight*." Review by Joshua Klein, *The Onion*.

"*White Palace*." Review by David Nusair, Reel Film Reviews, www.reelfilm.com.

"When Parallel Lives Converge." Kelly Carter, *USA Today*, September 17, 2002.

"Wicked Ways." Lisa Chambers, *TV Guide*, March 15-21, 2003.

"*The Witches of Eastwick*." Review by Jamieson Wolf Villeneuve, *The Green Man Review*, greenmanreview.com.

"A Woman of Substance." Melina Gerosa, *Ladies Home Journal*, November 1997.

"Well, maybe I am a bit of a maverick."

—Susan Sarandon

WEBSITES

The Internet Movie Data Base
www.imdb.com/Name?Sarandon+Susan.

This site contains a mini-biography of Susan Sarandon as well as information about her movies, nominations, and awards.

The Myelin Project
www.myelin.org

After appearing in *Lorenzo's Oil*, Susan Sarandon became spokesperson for The Myelin Project. A complete explanation of the project's important research and plans can be found on this site.

Princess Amanda's Shrine to Susan
www.geocities.com/sasarandon

One of Susan Sarandon's fans, Amanda Carneski owns and operates this colorful site, which is, of course, dedicated to her favorite actress.

Rotten Tomatoes
www.rottentomatoes.com/p/SusanSarandon-1013782

"Tomato ratings" for Sarandon's movies are listed here as well as links to the latest news articles about her.

The Susan Sarandon Site

www.chrisbaker.co.uk

Chris Baker established this comprehensive and enlightening unofficial fan site back in 1998. It continues to grow in content as well as in hits per day.

The Tim Robbins Universe

www.geocities.com/timrobbinsuniverse

"All Tim all the time," this unofficial fan site proclaims. But there's lots of information about Susan Sarandon here, too.

UNICEF

www.unicef.org/people/people_susan_sarandon.html

As part of her work with UNICEF, Susan Sarandon visited Tanzania. Results of her visit are included in this section of the organization's Internet presence.

SELECTED FILM REVIEWS

"In the arts, the critic is the only independent source of information. The rest is advertising."

—Pauline Kael

While not every film Susan Sarandon has appeared in came up to her high standards, many critics believe she enhanced the quality of almost all her movies—even when taking on small roles. The following reviews illustrate the level of respect Sarandon's acting talents have earned from a variety of film critics.

Moonlight Mile (2002)
by Kevin Laforest (for *Montreal Film Journal*)

This might be my favorite kind of film, one where you meet people you grow to know and care about, not because of cheap tricks but because the director has the good sense to let his characters live on screen. *Moonlight Mile* is the story of a young man who sticks around with his parents-in-law after his fiancée is murdered, but it's not a grim film. It's full of light and humor. In fact, it's not even about death; it's about life.

Writer-director Brad Silberling could have gone wrong a thou-
sand times with this premise, but he never does. This is not a manipulative tearjerker or a phony, idealistic family movie. Right from the
start, the impression the film gives is one of confidence. The hushed
down beauty of the images, the bittersweet tone.... This is a filmmaker who knows what he's doing. Silberling forgoes the whole first
act/introduction structure and dives right in. We're in a house with a
family, we see they're leaving for a funeral. No exposition is forced
on us. Silberling trusts us to connect the dots through the film. We
don't have to be told that it's set in the 70s, that Joseph was living
with the Floss family until he married their daughter, and that he's
sticking around because he feels this is the right thing to do.
Everything comes through naturally, like in real life.

I don't believe I've ever seen grief portrayed like this. Here, not
everyone is dressed in black, there are no constant crying fits, people
don't stop everything. They laugh, they go to work, they fall in love
again. Sure, there's this big hole inside of them, maybe they feel a bit
guilty, but they keep getting up in the morning anyway. They still have
their quirks and their bad habits, and their feelings take all sorts of
complicated forms. I know I'm being awfully vague, but this isn't a
film where you can pinpoint plot developments and character acts.
Therefore, at times I was unsure about the direction some things
were going, but again, Silberling makes you feel like you're in good
hands. It's in every musical cue (from Bob Dylan to Elton John to the
Rolling Stones track that gives the film its title), in the composition
of every shot: confidence.

And the acting! Susan Sarandon is almost always good, but here
she's just great. Her character is tough and funny, not the sobbing
mother you'd expect. I love how she takes it out on the friends and
neighbors who come to spout out cliché sympathies. I also love how
Dustin Hoffman and Sarandon interact. They're very convincing as
an old married couple who argue a lot but love each other anyway.
As for Jake Gyllenhaal, he's a nearly silent witness for most of the
film, but he's got the big blue eyes for that and this fits his character's
awkwardness at having to live with his late girlfriend's parents in a
strange town. Then there's Ellen Pompeo, who takes the very deli-

cate part of Gyllenhaal's new flame and manages not to make it feel insensitive.

Moonlight Mile is like *In the Bedroom* as Cameron Crowe might have directed it. I don't know if that sounds like a good deal to you, but it is. Don't miss it. (Released by Touchstone Pictures and rated "PG-13.")

Igby Goes Down (2002)
by Diana Saenger (for ReelTalk Movie Reviews)

In *Igby Goes Down*, Igby Slocumb (Kieran Culkin) has flunked out of more colleges than his wealthy mother (Susan Sarandon) can find for him. How she wishes he were more like his preppy brother (Ryan Phillippe), who is mastering his university classes, and life, just fine. Igby is determined to figure out what life is all about, and college or advice from his mother is not part of his plan.

After his mother once again steps in to do damage control at his latest college, Igby steals her credit card and takes off on his own. A host of interesting people either lend Igby a hand, offer advice, or take advantage of him. D. H., his godfather and his mother's good friend, always comes to the rescue. D. H. is played well by Jeff Goldblum, an actor noted for bringing amusing eccentricities of his own personality to his film characters. But instead of guiding Igby on a positive track, D. H. seems more interested in looking for his next affair. He deals with Igby by giving him a financial handout.

Sadly, there are few redeemable characters in this story. Igby himself engages in an affair with D. H.'s latest gal (Amanda Peet) and then takes up with another street urchin, Sookie (Claire Danes). Sookie, he feels, just might be the one to help him escape the web of dysfunctional family trappings that have ensnared him for so long.

Igby's father (Bill Pullman) has already checked out of reality and is in a mental home. And even when Igby and Oliver learn of their mother's cancer and impending death, it does little to change their sentiment about their mother. Although viewers never see most of the animosity about "mom" in this movie, the set-up of the film handles the unfolding drama in a believable fashion.

As Igby starts to reach for that olive branch of normalcy, he discovers Sookie has taken up with Oliver, once again proving he has no family allies. *Igby Goes Down* tries to prove that, under the surface, things are often not as they appear—but the movie offers nothing outstanding about Igby's coming-of-age journey.

And yet I enjoyed the film for its performances. Although Sarandon's role is short, she's always a trip. Phillippe doesn't have to stretch much as Oliver, and Danes's role is interesting, but I think she's unbelievable cast opposite Culkin. Pullman's performance as a mental patient impressed me with its intensity.

Still, it's Kieran Culkin I found most amazing to watch. Growing up in the Culkin clan under the shadow of his famous brother Macauley probably wasn't easy for a young man who wanted to perform as well. However, since his debut in *The Mighty* with Sharon Stone, Kieran has won over audiences and filmmakers with his fine work in films like *The Cider House Rules* and *The Dangerous Lives of Altar Boys*.

Igby Goes Down may not win any Oscar nominations, but I rate it as much better than most films now playing at the multiplexes. (Released by United Artists and rated "R" for language, sexuality, and drug content.)

Earthly Possessions (1999)
by Chris Baker (for The Susan Sarandon Site)

Based on Anne Tyler's acclaimed 1977 novel, which Steven Rogers adapted for television, *Earthly Possessions* is a bittersweet comedy about almost-lovers on the run, and the story is both slight and quirky. The film, shot outside New York City, was directed by James Lapine, the Tony Award-wining director of Stephen Sondheim's Broadway musicals *Sunday in the Park with George, Into the Woods,* and *Passion.*

As the film opens, gabby Charlotte Emory (Susan Sarandon), a discontented middle-aged housewife has decided to leave her husband (Jay O. Sanders), a stuffy and dull local minister. While she is waiting to withdraw cash at the bank in the very small town of Clarion, somewhere in the Southeast, a young man named Jake Simms Jr. (Stephen Dorff) grabs her and takes her hostage, demanding that the teller hand over all the money. It turns out to be only about $300 and the two misfits find themselves on the run. As they journey by car and bus down the eastern seaboard, the two fall in love. It's no surprise that they develop a mutual attraction or that Charlotte will consider this as a welcome departure from her everyday routine.

Like *Thelma & Louise*, it's the kind of story that can never end happily. The folks back in Clarion begin to suspect she is more of an accomplice than a hostage, unlikely as that may seem. Charlotte learns a lot about Jake: that he has a daffy pregnant girlfriend who is 17; that he is plagued with bad luck and bad judgment; that the father of the girl he impregnated declares he was "never out of trouble since the day he was born." But for Jake, Charlotte becomes something more than a lonely, sexually repressed chatterbox as well. And as played by Sarandon, with those fabulous eyes and that strange combination of assertiveness and vulnerability, she's uniquely poignant. She lies to Jake about having children, later admitting there was only a miscarriage and saying, "You never know how much you really want something until it's taken away."

Director Lapine has a gentle touch that is perfect for the material, and this is one comedy about small-town folks that doesn't make them all seem boobish or slow-witted. Lapine acknowledges the movie is quite different to the book, which concentrated more on Charlotte's family life. "It's definitely its own little animal," says Lapine, who likens it to an Alice in Wonderland-type fable. "These people kind of go down a rabbit hole and meet all of these eccentric types and come out the other end back to where they started." The plot, says Dorff, is more romance than caper. "It's not about the cops trying to find us. This is about two people. It's a character study." Those two people had a lot of charm for Sarandon. "They are so inept in their roles," she says of Charlotte and Jake. "He's such a bad bank robber and she's such a silly hostage. That is kind of what makes them funny."

Earthly Possessions marked Sarandon's first project for television since the 1986 CBS movie *Women of Valor*. It is said to be the prospect of doing a comedy after the emotionally wrenching demands of *Dead Man Walking* that drew her back to the small screen. "I liked the character and I liked that it was a little romantic, but still eccentric," she says. "It could be filmed in New York [where she and her family live] and it could be fun." Once she had signed on, it became a matter of finding someone who could bring Jake to life. "You can find people who are funny, you can find people who can be sexy and you can find people who are scary, but it's hard to find people who are all of them." But she agreed on Dorff after seeing his film work "He is confident, God knows, enough and experienced enough because he's been working for a long time."

Both Lapine and Dorff make no bones about the fact that they, like a lot of men, are in love with Sarandon. "I thought it would be great to work with her and it was great to work with her," says Lapine. "She is an amazing talent."

Cradle Will Rock (1999)
by Gabriel Shanks (for Mixed Reviews.net)

Tim Robbins is nothing if not impassioned. A sublime director of social mores, his films (*Bob Roberts*, *Dead Man Walking*) touch the emotional core underneath hot political buttons. His latest, *Cradle Will Rock*, is trademark Robbins, both a love letter to the theatre (where he began his career) and a pointed argument for support for the arts. Using a true but little known historic moment in the arts of the 20th century, Robbins has created an earnestly pleasing, shaggily loveable, and dramatically uneven movie. Like many films about the theatre, it is part paean, part romance, and 100% tribute.

It's too bad that the film only preaches to the converted. While theatre buffs like myself (I once wrote the beginnings of a play about the hero of *Cradle Will Rock*, tormented composer Marc Blitzstein) will recognize the import of adequate government funding and support of American artists without blinking twice, I'm not sure Robbins' film will change the minds of those opposed to arts funding. It often seems too inside, too clever for its own good. It extols the virtues of arts for the masses, then makes it seem like a wild party that you're not invited to. It laments the loss of the Federal Theatre Project, but shows its failings in the process.

If you don't know the Federal Theatre Project, it was part of Roosevelt's New Deal during the Depression. It offered low-cost theatre to millions of people, and put thousands of artists back to work at the same time. It also managed to turn a profit—quite a neat trick. Unfortunately, the Red Scare forced the FTP to close amid political maneuvers in Washington after only a few years. Today, the legacy is the rampant Republican idiocy that says art should only survive in the marketplace—a legacy that will garner us only lowest-common-denominator tripe like landscape paintings, Yanni, and Harlem Globetrotters in our museums, theatres, and galleries.

Watching *Cradle Will Rock*, it's all too easy to pull for the artists. They are heroes in this moment of Americana, after all. The history of Blitzstein's banned pro-union musical, *The Cradle Will Rock*, includes some of the greatest artists the world has ever seen. Orson Welles (a debauched Angus MacFayden) was the director, John Houseman (Cary Elwes) the producer. Robbins fashions a parallel story of the business giant Nelson Rockefeller (John Cusack) who commissions Diego Rivera (Ruben Blades) to paint an enormous mural in Rockefeller Center. (It was deemed too radical by Rockefeller upon completion, and completely destroyed.) Both storylines have a dynamic diva supporter: for Welles, Houseman and Blitzstein, it's the ebullient Countess (Vanessa Redgrave) who is as giddy as a schoolgirl around artists. Redgrave is scrumptiously over the top, charming even as she disobeys her husband (Philip Baker Hall) to go run with the heathens. Diego Rivera's diva is a delightfully hammy Margherita Sarfatti (Susan Sarandon), who charms the Americans even as she surreptitiously works for Mussolini.

When the Federal Theatre Project places a ban on all work the day before *The Cradle Will Rock* is to open, the artists stage a mini-revolt: they find another theatre and perform their play in spite of the ban (which could have cost them their jobs during the Depression). It's the film's most endearing moment, not surprisingly, and Blitzstein's brilliance shines through. The phrase "ahead of his time" could have been invented for him. At the same time, the film's other great story is being played out: the head of the FTP, Hallie Flanagan (Cherry Jones), is testifying before a Senate committee looking into Communist activity in government agencies. As her past is twisted by the senators to incriminate her and the FTP, Jones is a marvel. Her performance is one of the strongest in this rich, talented cast.

Less successful are subplots invented by Robbins, which drag the proceedings down to the level of the mundane. A street urchin-turned-star, Olive Stanton (Emily Watson), has a dull and pointless affair with her eventual leading man (Jamey Sheridan). A red-baiter (Joan Cusack) has a similarly head-scratching romance with the down-and-almost-out ventriloquist Tommy Crickshaw (Bill Murray, who seems to have been hired solely to lighten up the heavy proceedings.) Company actor Aldo Savano (John Turturro) has a number of battles with his pro-Italy, pro-Fascist family; the scenes have their hearts in the right place, but ultimately belong in another film altogether.

Like the year's other film that used the theatre as its subject (Turturro's own *Illuminata*), the most successful moments are the ones in the theatre itself. *Cradle Will Rock* aims to be a celebration of an art form AND an indictment of anti-arts sentiment. Tragically, that's just too large a burden to lay at the feet of what is essentially a light diversion. Robbins's film is engaging, interesting, and very enjoyable. But it won't change the world, the way the musical whose name it paraphrases did. Blitzstein, Rivera, Welles, and Houseman, I can't help thinking, would be disappointed with this well-made film. I suspect they'd want to redo it themselves.

Anywhere But Here (1999)
by Betty Jo Tucker (for ReelTalk Movie Reviews)

What a terrific idea! Cast Oscar winner Susan Sarandon (*Dead Man Walking*) and rising star Natalie Portman (*The Phantom Menace*) in a film together. Make it a comedy-drama about an outrageous mother and her more practical daughter. Recruit director Wayne Wang (*The Joy Luck Club*) to helm the project. Put all this together and what do you have? An exceptional movie titled *Anywhere But Here*.

Wang has a passion for and skill in telling stories about women and families. "My wife says I was probably a woman in a past life," the filmmaker recalls with a laugh. "She says that I have a certain sensibility for and understanding of women. Also, the Chinese believe that we have both yin and yang sides; perhaps I'm more in touch with my yin side, which is the feminine side."

Wang's sensibilities make him the perfect one to transfer Mona Simpson's novel about a volatile mother-daughter relationship to the big screen. Screenwriter Alvin Sargent's strong insights into the American family also contribute to the movie's humanistic tone. (Remember his great script for *Ordinary People*?)

While *Anywhere But Here* tells a simple story, it deals with important concepts like dependence, independence, love, and hate. Ann August (Portman) doesn't want to move from her small hometown to a big city. But her mother Adele (Sarandon) thinks her dreams of a better life for both of them will never come true if they stay in Bay City, Wisconsin. As the two adjust to a new life in Los Angeles, their relationship changes and evolves.

Because the success of this film depends on its two stars, would it be as entertaining without Sarandon and Portman? Probably not. Like the Mona Lisa, Sarandon gets more valuable as she ages. She brings her own brand of excitement to any role. Besides being a consummate dramatic actress, she shows a wonderful flair for comedy here. Explaining the eccentric character she plays, Sarandon points out, "I think what's interesting about Adele is that she's doing all the wrong things for all the right reasons. She loves her daughter, but is misguided and self-serving."

Although Ann loves her mother deeply, she can't stand Adele most of the time. "Even when she's ruining my life, there's something about my mother," the young girl confesses as she goes off to college. "There's romance and a sense of power. When she dies, the world will be dull and flat."

Portman's innate grace and intelligence shine through in her portrayal of the daughter. Sarandon insists the casting of Portman was critical to understanding the mother-daughter relationship. She's absolutely correct in believing when viewers see the smart and healthy Portman, they have to say, "Well, for all the mom's silliness and mistakes, she must be doing something right because Ann is a great kid."

Moviegoers who enjoy good human-interest stories should not miss this film. But, those in the mood for action scenes, violence, car chases, and special effects will have to look anywhere but here. (Released by Fox 2000 Pictures and rated "PG-13" for sex-related material.)

Stepmom (1998)
by Susan Granger, SSG Syndicate (for www.susangranger.com)

Bring along lots of handkerchiefs because this adult drama with that terrible title is a real weeper. It's about two women who hate each other, two kids caught in the middle, and one man just trying to survive. Ed Harris's divorced wife, Susan Sarandon, and their kids—who live in suburbia—are anything but happy when his perky photographer girlfriend, Julia Roberts, moves into his Manhattan apartment. Everyone hates her until a life-threatening illness (cancer) forces Sarandon to accept her ex-husband's fiancée.

Both women are selfish in their own way. There's the perfect "soccer mom" who values her children's well-being over everything else versus the surrogate, unwanted step-parent who never wanted children and is far more interested in her career than raising a family.

Grasping her dynamic, gritty part and running with it magnificently, Susan Sarandon's mean, bitchy portrayal could earn her the

Best Actress Academy Award this year with fresh, hip Julia Roberts claiming the Best Supporting Actress prize. Their scenes are so true and so vital and cut so deep. The moving script by Gigi Levangie— "I am a stepmom. I wrote this from personal experience."—and Ron Bass—*Rain Man, My Best Friend's Wedding*—is juicy, relevant, and contemporary. Director Chris Columbus (*Home Alone, Mrs. Doubtfire*) expertly adds bite and heart to the rich texture, making it about the humanity of people with all the laughter and tears of real families.

On the Granger Movie Gauge of 1 to 10, *Stepmom* is a spellbinding 10. It's a "must-see" to watch two extraordinary actresses ignite the screen with bravura, Oscar-caliber performances in a poignant celebration of family and of life.

Twilight (1998)
by Chris Baker (for The Susan Sarandon Site)

You can't fault the pedigree. Three Oscar winners out front and a gathering of the best supporting actors money can buy. Shot in the naturalistic L.A. hues of brown and yellow, *Twilight* ducks and weaves about its plot. To capture the atmosphere of old Hollywood, much of the film was shot at the art-deco mansion of Cedric Gibons, the legendary head of the MGM art department in the 1930s.

Veteran private investigator Harry Ross (Paul Newman) is living at the home of cancer stricken movie star Jack Ames (Gene Hackman) and his wife (Susan Sarandon), a femme fatale hiding a sordid secret. The crinkly gumshoe exposes a crime far too close to home for comfort. After he accepts a delivery job from at-death's-door Jack, it is Ross who pries open the requisite can-of-worms. You know the score—blackmail, murder, the cops slightly off the pace. This is pure Chandler, with Newman's sandpaper vocals sharpening up some snappy dialogue.

The film presents characters that are, depending on your point of view, either classic or cliché, including a very nice turn from Garner. The shadowy showdowns twist and turn until a 20-year-old body is exhumed and it's a short hop to picking which of the major players plugged the victim.

It's a pleasure to watch such heavyweights hold the screen together—the lead trio present the awkward mannerisms of the decaying heart with cool subtlety.

Illuminata (1998)
by Susan Granger, SSG Syndicate (for www.susangranger.com)

After *Shakespeare in Love*, this sumptuously presented but overly long story of behind-the-scenes actors pales in comparison. But you have to credit it as a labor of love by John Turturro, who co-wrote, directed, and acted in it. Set amid a flamboyant turn-of-the-century New York repertory company, it revolves around a failing resident playwright, Turturro, whose claim to fame is his marriage to the troupe's leading lady, played by Katherine Borowitz, Turturro's real-life wife.

The playwright yearns to shelve the heavy-handed melodramas of the period as he aspires to a more naturalistic style of theater, but no one believes in him. *Illuminata* is both the title of a play-within-the-movie and what he eventually calls his wife after they survive treachery, backbiting, and intrigue—not to mention the on-stage death of the leading man mid-performance on opening night.

Susan Sarandon is glorious as the promiscuous, aging diva who glances at a young actress and murmurs, "That is how I shall look years from now. I'm beginning to be able to play ingénues." But Christopher Walken steals the picture as a smug, gay critic—think Oscar Wilde—who relishes the cruelty he liberally dishes out, and Bill Irwin is amusing as the wretchedly reluctant object of his affections. Their characterizations are particularly bawdy. Beverly D'Angelo, Ben Gazzara, and the late Donal McCann complete the supporting cast, along with Turturro's son and cousin. On the Granger Movie Gauge of 1 to 10, *Illuminata* is an art-house 6, exploring the durability of love with enough dramatic lulls to catch a quick snooze.

Dead Man Walking (1995)
by Kathleen Carroll (for *Film Scouts*)

The prison chaplain warns Sister Helen Prejean she should not expect the impending execution of a convicted killer to be like "a James Cagney movie." He has a point. Cagney, you will recall, bristled with indignation as he walked to the electric chair in one of his most memorable performances. By contrast what makes Tim Robbins's *Dead Man Walking* such a riveting, profoundly moving experience is its unflinching realism.

Hollywood has traditionally made heroes out of bad guys but that does not happen here. Matthew Poncelet, the death row inmate in this particular case, display's Cagney's defiantly unrepentant attitude at first. But he soon confesses that he's scared. So is his spiritual advisor Sister Helen. A compassionate New Orleans nun, she finds herself publicly condemned for her decision to stick by Poncelet. But she persists in what becomes a fierce struggle to save his life and his soul. "I'm just trying to follow the example of Jesus, who said that every person is worth more than their worst act," says Sister Helen in explaining her actions.

Using Sister Helen Prejean's 1993 true-life book as his inspiration, Robbins more than confirms his talent as both a screenwriter and a director. That Robbins would even dare to make a movie about a spiritual journey such as this shows remarkable courage. To his credit, Robbins presents a carefully balanced view of capital punishment, revealing the true complexity of this highly emotional issue.

Although Poncelet is facing the supposedly more humane method of death by lethal injection, the actual procedure seems like nothing less than cold-blooded murder. The convicted murderer is gently protective of his mother and younger brothers and the viewer inevitably feels sympathy for his family in the poignant scene in which they say their good-byes.

Even more heartbreaking are the shattered parents of the teenage lovers whom Poncelet continues to maintain he did not kill. The parents, not surprisingly, want revenge and Sister Helen is forced to deal with their understandable rage. There are also chilling flashbacks of the crime itself—a double murder of such casual brutality it reinforces the parents' demands for the death penalty.

Susan Sarandon's unadorned face accurately mirrors the inner strength and momentary doubts of Sister Helen. She gives a remarkably sensitive performance. Sean Penn transforms Poncelet into a compelling full-bodied character whose brash arrogance is slowly stripped away.

Dead Man Walking demonstrates the power of love in a way that is absolutely unforgettable, making it easily one of the best movies of 1995.

The Client (1994)
by Joan Ellis (An Illusion Review for www.joanellis.com)

Hollywood has learned how to handle John Grisham. Take his annual bestseller, shower it with talent and money, and the mediocrity of his material will drown in the glitz of the big production. *The Client* has Susan Sarandon and Tommy Lee Jones, two stars who are so interesting to watch that you forget the story is a sieve.

Would you bet on this plot? A 12-year-old boy sneaks off for a smoke in the woods and witnesses the suicide of a Mafia lawyer after he tells the boy where the very important box is buried. The boy finds himself a lawyer who, while a recovering alcoholic, managed in three years to finish law school and collect the experience and wisdom to take on the state's famed prosecutor, who wants to be governor. You would if you had Sarandon and Jones as your protagonists.

The movie cuts jarringly back and forth between two worlds: the dangerous one where Reggie (Sarandon) joins her child client in playing detective, and the slightly safer courtroom that is the battlefield for Reggie and Roy Foltrigg (Jones). Their jousting is mediated by Judge Harry Roosevelt (Ossie Davis), whose favoritism toward Reggie is a welcome safe haven for her and for the audience, but extravagantly inappropriate by any normal standard. Roy wants the boy's testimony, Reggie wants his love, and the mob wants him dead.

That puts Mark in the lead role, quite a load for a new young actor, Brad Renfro, to carry. If Renfro plays it a little too wise and too smart, it's not surprising since he is asked to be the primary care-taker of his mother, his younger brother, and his lawyer. Mary Louise Parker, as Mark's mother, conveys beautifully and mournfully the despair of a woman who cannot help her family or herself.

As Roy Foltrigg, Tommy Lee Jones uses his innate subtleties to create a character that you can love one minute for the honor you hope lies beneath the smarm, and hate the next for the opportunis-tic manipulation of the media on his march to the statehouse.

Susan Sarandon's Reggie is astonishing in her vulnerability. The audience must live with the probability that her professional veneer may dissolve at any moment. She infuses the part with such quiet intelligence that it is impossible to concentrate on anything else—like John Grisham's bad plot—when she's on screen.

Sunk in my seat and contemplating my annoyance at the holes in this movie, I remembered the case on the nightly news: bloody gloves, daggers, throat slittings, wailing dogs, and victimized children alternating with courtroom scenes of Robert Shapiro, the master media-manipulator, and Marcia Clark, the taut, confident prosecutor. So *The Client* is no less real than life. Enjoy it for the tension and the gloss. It has Jones and Sarandon: a bad plot couldn't get a better break. (Released by Warner Bros. and rated "PG-13.")

Safe Passage (1994)
by Joan Ellis (An Illusion Review for www.joanellis.com)

Safe Passage is a movie lover's best surprise: an unheralded film with zip. It is the story of Mag (Susan Sarandon) and Patrick (Sam Shepard), who have raised seven grown sons and are separated—worn down, it seems, by the grand effort.

Mag is in her second decade of erasure, just when a woman's soul begins to scream, "Enough!" She will not watch one more time as Patrick dunks his tea bag seven times and throws it over his shoulder into the kitchen sink. It's just such things as tea bags that trigger big emotions in women at the end of the in-house phase of family life.

For Mag, who has mothering in her bones, the on-their-own phase is even more harrowing than the earlier years of just keeping them alive. On this particular night, in a routine familiar to her family, she wakes up in a nightmare that something is wrong with one of her sons. Which one? A series of marvelous flashbacks show Mag as a primal protector of her young. No football collision or mad dog on a paper route ever modified her visceral response.

The family members gather to wait for news of the threatened son, and by the time resolution comes, we know them very well. The boys know their mother will cover her fear by turning up Mazursky's "Pictures from an Exhibition" to full volume. One of them, a veterinarian, will spend the visit tracking his father's periodic bouts of blindness. In a time of crisis, the predictability of the parents' behavior and their sons' knowing ways of handling it are drawn at once with subtlety and exaggeration—a neat trick.

After an hour or so, we care about all of these people, from Simon, the 13-year-old youngest to Alfred, the oldest. The reason we care is that writer Deena Goldstone has written a script (based on the novel by Ellyn Bache) that is laced with good lines that reveal character. Give good lines to a good cast, and the rest is pleasure.

Susan Sarandon makes Mag a revelation of motherhood itself. From "I was 35 before I had a dinner where I wasn't cutting someone else's meat" to "Percy, you're absent from your own life, and you're breaking my heart," she's the mother whose children are part of her soul.

Nick Stahl is simply terrific. He acts with quiet grace at a very young age, making Simon a subtle mix of adolescence and filial love. Sam Shepard, still a man of few words, is fine as the man who drives his wife crazy by not understanding her turmoil. Robert Sean Leonard is very warm as Alfred, the organized eldest son who tries vainly to bring order to his family's chaos.

The movie's strength is that the resolution becomes secondary to the touching, very funny portrait of a family. It's a heart tugger with belly laughs. What a difference a scriptwriter makes. (Released by New Line Cinema and rated PG-13.)

Lorenzo's Oil (1992)
by Chris Hicks (for Deseret News)

Susan Sarandon dominates *Lorenzo's Oil* as the ultimate nurturing mother out to save her child. But in this case, it's a seemingly futile rescue effort, since the child is under attack by an unseen and virtually unknown enemy, a disease that is too rare and too new to adequately comprehend, and therefore not very high on the priority list of medical investigation.

Sarandon is fearless in her performance, not at all afraid to make her character appear so single-minded that she is often curt and occasionally downright obnoxious. It's a wide-ranging role, played to the hilt, and Sarandon would seem to be a sure thing in the coming Oscar race.

Lorenzo's Oil is a true story, a case study of parental love as Augusto and Michaela Odone (Nick Nolte and Sarandon) refuse to roll over and let their child suffer without a fight.

The film begins in 1983 as 5-year-old Lorenzo (Zack O'Malley Greenburg) is initially misdiagnosed. But as time passes, his parents become certain that the boy's wild mood swings and the sudden development of self-destructive habits are due to an illness the doctors simply cannot pinpoint.

The disease is eventually identified as adrenoleukodystrophy, referred to as ALD, which is inherited by young boys from their mothers, who are merely carriers, and causes gradual degeneration until the patient dies, usually within two years of being diagnosed. The Odones enlist the aid of a well-intentioned but ineffectual doctor (Peter Ustinov) who specializes in ALD. But they soon become frustrated with his hesitant approach, though they allow Lorenzo to become involved in experimental treatment. It isn't long, however, before the Odones relinquish their passive approach for a more aggressive tack.

Augusto begins spending hours in libraries, poring over medical journals, looking for anything that might hint at a cure. Meanwhile, Michaela spends every waking moment tending to her deteriorating child's needs, fighting off guilt at having been the carrier of this dreaded disease.

They find themselves battling both doctors and other parents of ALD children as they pursue their goal, and after some years they do begin to make some progress. They help develop a compound, the title oil, which will stave off some symptoms and point toward hope for the future. Ultimately, the ending cannot be a "happy" one, but it is certainly filled with optimism.

Directed and co-written by Australian George Miller (the Mad Max films, *The Witches of Eastwick*), who is a medical doctor as well as a filmmaker. *Lorenzo's Oil* is meticulous storytelling, evenly paced and filled with detail. There is also a depth of character here and an intelligence that are missing from disease-of-the-week television movies that tackle subjects like this.

The performances are all first-rate, including the six children (led by young Greenburg) who play Lorenzo at various stages of his life. Nolte's affected Italian accent takes some getting used to, but the film is so involving and his performance so compelling that after a while it doesn't really matter. And it's very nice to see Ustinov again after too long an absence from the big screen.

The real knockout here, however, is Sarandon, who is absolutely riveting. She's every bit as wrenching, touching, and fulfilling as the film itself. And that's saying something. (Released by Universal Pictures and rated "PG-13" for some language, though it is obviously too intense for young children.)

Light Sleeper (1991)
by Walter Chaw (for ReelTalk Movie Reviews)

With his large hands and gaunt features, Willem Dafoe invests "I've been having trouble sleeping lately" with the melancholy heft of cathedral bells. *Light Sleeper* touches on writer/director Paul

Schrader's obsessions with addiction, alien sexuality, and marooned anti-heroes tenuously anchored by the unreciprocated love for an unattainable woman. But it lilts with a sort of jazz that's largely missing from the rest of his stripped down work, a product of a solemn score by Michael Been and of cinematographer Edward Lachmann's affinity for the disconnected urban tableaus of Edward Hopper. The film is Schrader's most beautiful by far, with scenes set along haunted noir city streets, empty green apartments, icy blue morgues, and the shades of brown layering Dafoe's aptly named sojourner, John LeTour.

A drug mule for high-class dealer Ann (Susan Sarandon), John spends the first part of *Light Sleeper* moving in and out of the sleeping metropolis like a vampire, dispensing nepenthe to Ann's carefully cultivated clientele. A murder occurs in Central Part, in the background of the piece, and it isn't until the second half of the film that this murder becomes current in John's life, and the life of his ex-wife Marianne (Dana Delany) with whom he's trying to reconcile. Addiction being often dealt with in film, the thing that astounds about *Light Sleeper* is that in what is Schrader's most overtly noir piece he approaches addiction from the perspective of the doomed hopes of a recovering junkie. The film moves like a dream—a late reveal of Marianne in a degraded state the sort of feverish hallucinations that would have only a fraction of the impact were it not for Schrader's meticulous structure, and for Dafoe's heartbreaking and understated performance.

Two conversations (between John and Marianne, between John and Ann) are separated by columns and planes—distancing the players in a way that is affecting and lonesome while functioning like bookends for the picture: milestones for John as first the detective of the past, then the penitent patient for the future. Its conclusion is the kind of cathartic bloodbath of the Schrader-scripted *Taxi Driver*; it moves through *Light Sleeper* like a tired exhalation into a tenor saxophone, marking the film as deeply problematic in that it is at once nihilistic and genuinely hopeful. Dafoe, Schrader's favorite collaborator, with his winsome vulnerability brought to the fore (and explored with a surprising sympathy by Schrader) is the perfect fit for the picture's schizophrenia—and simply extraordinary. There is a matter-of-factness about him that plays well with Sarandon's unaffected turn as a businesswoman trafficking in an illicit business. That *Light Sleeper* is deeply flawed is without question, that it approaches for long moments the fugue state of insomnia and hopelessness forgives a multitude of sins.

Thelma & Louise (1991)
by Chris Baker (for The Susan Sarandon Site)

Hailed by critics as a feminist manifesto for the 90s, Ridley Scott's *Thelma & Louise* is a genuine must-see for its breathless, epic realization of a smart, funny script and bravura performances from its wonderful leading ladies, Susan Sarandon and Geena Davis.

This entertaining, giddy tale of two friends who become fugitives is not that original—screenwriter Callie Khouri couldn't have concocted this movie without *Butch Cassidy and the Sundance Kid*'s pattern for an action adventure about comically wisecracking comrades. But it works because of the astonishing fact that this is the first big-budget Hollywood picture in which the pals are gals.

And what gals! When Geena Davis's bullied housewife Thelma and Sarandon's worn waitress Louise sneak off for a quiet weekend break from their many cares (synonymous with their men), a drunken, foul-mouthed, would-be rapist in the car park of a honkytonk sparks Louise's pent-up rage and memories of past abuses.

One unthinking, split-second of violence later, and the sickened, terrified women are on the run across the Southwest from a murder charge. That their route to freedom and fulfillment goes way over the top in a Bonnie and Bonnie scenario of escalating disaster and crime is less troublesome than it ought to be, thanks to Davis and Sarandon raising hell and wisecracking with wild, womanly, utterly captivating style.

For a change, the actors trailing in their wake get to be the stooges: Thelma's repulsive husband, Louise's Peter Pan unable-to-commit fella, Plod of the FBI, the Nazi redneck cop, the lewd trucker, and the seductive thug. Even Harvey Keitel's comprehending detective is paternalistic in his sympathy for the women.

One cannot but share these women's exultation as they answer "the call of the wild," speeding along the highway in a convertible T-bird, chugging Wild Turkey, swapping delightful one-liners and harmonizing with the radio.

Scott has created a visual sensation using the stunning and desolate landscape of the U. S. Southwest as a mythic backdrop for the women's daring odyssey.

What really makes this buddy movie a true hear-in-the-mouth job is that when Butch and Sundance went out they were holding guns. When Thelma and Louise are indelibly freeze-framed, pedal to the metal in their crazy act of defiance, they are holding hands.

White Palace (1990)
by David Nusair (for Reel Film Reviews, www.reelfilm.com)

In *White Palace*, James Spader plays a variation on the type of role that made him famous: the yuppie. This time, he's a yuppie mourning the loss of his wife. He's got a great job and some good friends, but something's missing from his life. One day, though, he meets an earthy waitress at the local hamburger joint and the two begin an unusual and illicit romance.

The earthy woman is, of course, played by Susan Sarandon. I say "of course" because this is the perfect Sarandon role. She gets to do everything she's good at—there's comedy, drama, pretty much everything an actor would crave in a role. She's very good here, as is Spader.

Their problems arise, then, when Spader begins introducing Sarandon to his friends and family. Spader, being an upper crust sort of fellow, has friends of a similar ilk. And not surprisingly, they all react to Sarandon pretty much the same way that the shopkeeper reacted to Julia Roberts in *Pretty Woman*. It must be said, though, that the screenplay doesn't embarrass itself by having the reaction be as one-dimensional as in *Pretty Woman*. The characters do attempt to be polite to Sarandon, but the problem is they have nothing in common, so it just comes off looking like they're being rude and obnoxious to her.

What I like, nay admired, about *White Palace* is the way it made the over-40 Sarandon look as attractive as most movies would make a 20-year-old look (well, as long as you don't count the pit hair. That's just gross.) This is a realistic look at an older (or bolder, if you want to listen to the tagline) woman who's still sexy and knows it. It's rare you find such a sensuous role for a woman as old as Sarandon—usually once actresses hit forty, they're relegated to teacher and motherly roles—and Sarandon certainly has the looks and the chops to pull off the performance.

Ditto Spader. He's as good as ever playing the slightly trepidatious yuppie-in-mourning. The supporting cast is irrelevant; this is Sarandon and Spader's movie. However, I found a subplot (mercifully short, at least) involving Sarandon's estranged sister to be tiresome and unnecessary. She's supposed to be some sort of a psychic, so obviously, there's a scene in which she reveals that Spader is deeply hurt because of his dead wife. No kidding, Sherlock. This subplot could have easily been excised, as it offers nothing relevant to the movie.

Despite that little qualm, *White Palace* is certainly worth seeking out. It's a love story that feels realistic (unlike the shiny and entirely-too-slick teen romances that are all the rage nowadays) and whose characters will not soon be forgotten.

Bull Durham (1988)
by John Larsen (for Lightviews.com)

Bull Durham is a romantic comedy about America's other favorite pastime. The first is baseball, but there's plenty to root for on and off the field in writer-director Ron Shelton's extremely enjoyable debut. Before stepping behind the camera as a director, Shelton had written numerous films and served as a second unit director. When Shelton decided he was ready to helm his first film, he penned this engaging tale of a minor league baseball team and the women in their lives.

As Shelton relates in the DVD's running audio commentary, movies with a sports theme were considered poison at the box office. The film was turned down twice by every major studio, and when Orion finally decided to make the film, they only gave him $5 million. Well, it's amazing what a little ingenuity and a lot of passion can do with $5 million. *Bull Durham* may take place in the minor leagues, but the film is Major League all the way. It features winning performances, one of the brightest, snappiest romantic comedy scripts ever, and assured direction. It all comes together in a fun-filled, deeply romantic good time that even makes foul balls something to cheer about.

Kevin Costner is sensational as Crash Davis, a seasoned player now making his home with the Durham Bulls. Davis, who once spent 21 days in the "Show," knows he's just biding his time when he arrives at the Bull's Clubhouse. He's there to make hotshot pitcher "Nuke" Laloosh (Tim Robbins) look good, which proves to be more of a headache than a task.

Davis has his eye on team handler Annie Savoy (Susan Sarandon, who just oozes sex in this film), who in turn has her eye on Nuke. Annie's knowledge of the game and her penchant for taking hot prospects under her wing and into her bed make her a major asset to the team. "There's never been a ballplayer who slept with me who didn't have the best year of his career."

Thanks to Annie and Crash, Nuke matures into a major league threat, and finally gets a shot at the "Show." That leaves Annie and Crash with some time to explore their feelings for each other, which leads to one of the most romantic interludes on film. The leads are exceptional, and they get great assists from a well-balanced supporting cast, including the wonderful Trey Wilson as the manager of the team and Robert Wuhl as the coach. There are so many memorable moments in *Bull Durham*. Add them up and what you get is a great film that proves movies with a sports theme can succeed at the box office. Of course, it helps to have stars like Costner, Sarandon, and Robbins, who all ooze charm in every scene.

The Witches of Eastwick (1987)
by Jamieson Wolf Villeneuve (for ReelTalk Movie Reviews)

In *The Witches of Eastwick*, three bored New England women take center stage for a whimsical adventure based on John Updike's best-seller of the same name. Portrayed by Michelle Pfeiffer, Cher and Susan Sarandon, this high-powered trio helps turn Updike's unusual tale of cavorting with the devil into an enjoyable cinematic romp.

The devil, in this case, is Daryl van Horne (Jack Nicholson), who moves into Eastwick with designs on all three of the women in question. To seduce them, Daryl gives each of these best friends the thing she desires the most. This "average horny little devil," as he calls himself, bestows his special magic on cellist Jane (Sarandon), single mother/columnist Sukie (Pfeiffer) and sculptor Alex (Cher).

After accidentally conjuring up their ideal man in the form of Jack Nicholson, all three women are drawn to him by his uncanny ability to bring out their wild sides. Who can forget, for example, the "cello lesson" he gives Sarandon's character, or the way he sweet-talks Cher into staying when she wants to leave?

Things start to fall apart when Felicia (Veronica Cartwright), the self-appointed moral arbiter of Eastwick society, becomes unhinged as a result of Daryl's shenanigans. Cartwright (*The Birds*) is simply terrific in this role. She's quite convincing as a worried prophet who's certain she's battling true Evil. Unfortunately, no one will listen to Felicia—not even her husband—because of her outrageous behavior.

Jane, Sukie and Alex soon begin to wonder who Daryl might be. Is he really the Devil? Is he practicing voodoo? They actually don't know much of anything about their mystery man, but they know they must get away from him. How to do that is the big challenge for them.

When they try to flee from his clutches, Daryl punishes them all with their worst fears. He gives Sukie pain; Alex gets snakes; and Jane ages rapidly. Convinced that Daryl would do great harm to them if they ever left him, the women now understand the seriousness of their situation. Then, when all three of Daryl's sexy trio become pregnant at the same time, they finally decide to get revenge by using their new magical powers against him.

Devil he may be, but Daryl van Horne has taught these witches some awesome tricks, and they have to use every one of them to give him his comeuppance and survive the ordeal.

The Witches of Eastwick is an incredible achievement and an amazing movie. My personal favorite is Cher, with her smart talk, sassy smile and interesting fashion sense. Jack Nicholson portrays the Devil as only he can, loudly and with plenty of anger and spice. Susan Sarandon is refreshing as a sexy femme fatale, and it was unusual for her to take on such a comedic role at this point in her career. But she is superb, as is Michelle Pfeiffer playing her journalist role with enough innocence and naiveté to make everyone like her. The ensemble cast works extremely well; all of the actors play off each other with not one person out of place.

One of the reasons the movie works so well is because it portrays witches as normal women who possess power. It speaks to the idea that everyone has mojo, juice or whatever you want to call it. It's just that some are more able to tap into it than others. Sure, there are special effects and fancy movie magic, but you never forget for one minute that the three main characters are just ordinary women who happen to have power.

I must have watched this movie thirty times, but I can still find something to enjoy about it each and every time. It is a piece of genius, a wonderful film. It flawlessly combines reality with magic, painting a picture that anyone would give their eyeteeth to own. It works well on many levels. It's comedic, smart and sassy. The women in this movie aren't weak little things who whine and complain about how hard their life is (which they do in the book). They are independent women, proud of their sexual side. The movie takes a look at sex under the cover of magic and shows that everyone is entitled to a little exploration.

The Witches of Eastwick also tries to portray modern witchcraft in a positive light. Now of course this is Hollywood and there are a few things that just couldn't happen (i.e. flying—if any witch out there can do that, would you please let me know), but for the most part the magic is kept simple and easy to understand. No complicated rituals here. Someone obviously did their research.

This is a rare treat of a film, a diamond in the rough and full of excellent performances. If you haven't seen *The Witches of Eastwick* in a few years, it's time you watched it again.

Atlantic City (1980)
by Betty Jo Tucker (for ReelTalk Movie Reviews)

On the Boardwalk in *Atlantic City*, so the old song goes, "life can be peaches and cream." Not so for Sally Matthews, a wannabe croupier with a philandering husband, nor for Lou Pasco, an old-time hood now reduced to taking care of an elderly Betty Grable look-alike.

When Sally (Susan Sarandon) and Lou (Burt Lancaster) meet after a dope deal by Sally's husband goes bad, each has something the other needs. Longing to be the important *Atlantic City* crime figure he was in the past (or was he?), Lou sees Sally and the money from the drug caper as his way back to glory. Sally, much younger than Lou but not immune to his considerable charm, wants him "to teach her stuff" so she can deal her way to Monte Carlo.

Because of their outstanding performances, Lancaster (*Elmer Gantry*) and Sarandon (*Pretty Baby*) made me really care about Lou and Sally. I wanted their dreams to come true. I shared their pain as I watched them being attacked by vicious hoods and forced to leave *Atlantic City*. Lou hadn't been out of *Atlantic City* for 20 years, so he evoked my strongest sympathy.

Atlantic City itself plays a key role in this critically acclaimed Louis Malle (*Pretty Baby*) film—fom an early-on building demolition shot to scenes inside the casinos and on the Boardwalk. Like Sally and Lou, the city is going through changes; the old is giving way to the new. Entertainer Robert Goulet's (*I'd Rather Be Rich*) cameo scene serves as a not-so-subtle reminder of how our senses can be dulled during periods of transition.

Although *Atlantic City* is a serious drama, noted playwright John Guare (*The House of Blue Leaves*) adds a few humorous surprises to his intelligent screenplay. For example, after Lou makes all the funeral arrangements for Sally's husband, Sally asks, "Why are you doing this for me?" Lou answers pretentiously, "Sinatra gives wings to hospitals. We all do what we can do." In another amusing scene, Lou tries to impress Sally with his criminal past by telling her that "casinos are too wholesome for me."

Earning her first Oscar nomination, Sarandon displays an almost ethereal beauty as the ambitious Sally. Her sexy lemon-wash sequence is unforgettable, her acting impeccable. Combining wide-eyed naiveté with an edgy sensual appeal, she finally comes into her own as a first-rate actress. But it's Lancaster who owns *Atlantic City*. His remarkable interpretation of the sometimes pathetic, always elegant Lou Pasco emerges as pure movie magic and earned the legendary actor his last, but definitely well-deserved, Oscar nomination. (Released by Paramount Pictures.)

Pretty Baby (1978)
by Frank Wilkins (for ReelTalk Movie Reviews)

1917. America is contemplating sending soldiers to the battlefields of Europe; radio is not yet available as the entertainment medium of choice for Americans; and prostitution runs rampant in the Storyville District of New Orleans, Louisiana. One particular establishment, run by the astute but sassy Nell (Frances Faye) is the setting of the opening scene of *Pretty Baby*. We see the 12-year-old Violet (Brooke Shields) as she is watching her mother, Hattie (Susan Sarandon) apparently satisfy a John, but as the camera pans, we see that Hattie is actually in the middle of childbirth—surely one of the less desirable byproducts of her profession.

From this opening scene on, director Louis Malle pulls us into the seedy and repugnant life of Violet as she grows up and becomes a young lady within the walls of a household completely devoid of morals, chastity, and self-respect. Despite the disturbing subject matter, Malle's sophisticated hand gives us the ability to view Violet with a fatherly concern rather than an immaterial disgust. We see the world through her eyes as he holds the camera on her face, allowing us to completely take in her thoughts and emotions. What will become of a young girl who has seen and done such things?

The frequent visits to Nell's Place by a photographer named Bellocq (Keith Carradine) catch the eye of Violet. She's envious of Bellocq's attention towards her mother although his interest lies in capturing her grace and beauty on film rather than in pleasures of the flesh. Bellocq eventually becomes attracted to Violet's precious, gem-like beauty and wisdom beyond her years. The two marry, but we are never convinced of Bellocq's love for Violet. It seems to be a marriage more out of concern for her well-being than a marriage of passion and infatuation. In a very moving scene, Bellocq buys her a doll and she asks why. "Because every little girl should have a doll," he replies. Violet's reaction is brilliant. She is angered that he still thinks of her as a child, but she can't resist the urge to play with the doll.

Carradine gives a memorable performance as Bellocq. His cool demeanor allows him to slowly become the hero we hope can eventually end the madness. A house full of petty whores, drug-users, cheating Senators and businessmen, and other irreputables is no place for a child to be raised. And Bellocq convinces us that he can save this poor girl from despair.

Sarandon, as Hattie, is seamless and flawless, not to mention at her shapeliest best. She delivers a very textured performance as a mother torn between the love of her children, the struggle to succeed, and the need for caring and support. Nell's is a place to give love, not receive it and her ticket out is marriage to a millionaire. She loves the camera as it pauses for long periods on her face and nude body. Her role consists of several multi-faceted characteristics: mother, model, wife, and businesswoman, yet she convinces us in each one.

The task asked of Brooke Shields is a mighty one, especially being a young model with little acting experience. Violet is tragically suspended somewhere between pre-pubescence and adulthood yet Malle capitalizes on Brooke's screen presence and beautifully innocent charm to present the story as an expose of a decadent era rather than the sexuality of a 12-year-old girl.

I was constantly expecting a tragic event to go down but it never really does. I finally realized that the tragedy was the situation itself. *Pretty Baby* is a dark and disturbing look at a lifestyle that was probably not too uncommon in the days of legal bordellos and non-existent birth control. Malle and co-writer Polly Platt have carefully revealed the tale of a young girl's coming of age in a lifestyle we don't want to know exists. They feed us with just enough information to finish out Violet's life according to our own hopes, desires, and emotions.

The Rocky Horror Picture Show (1975)
by Joshua Vasquez (for ReelTalk Movie Reviews)

"It's not easy having a good time; even smiling makes my face ache," the luxuriously perverse yet decadently wounded Dr. Frank-N-Furter says at one point near the end of *The Rocky Horror Picture Show*, and that sentiment could be seen as the ultimate truth at the heart of the film. *Rocky Horror* has become a cultural phenomena, having acquired the aura of a "lived" experience more than merely a "watched" one; the evolution of the film into a "midnight movie" cult has transformed the relationship between viewer and film into a procession of textual give and take. *Rocky Horror* has formed its own sub-societal order of loyal followers who drape themselves in the folds of the film's own air of manic theatrical display, and through this transformation, the film becomes something more than entertainment.

Beneath the campy comedic gestures and genre spoofing, which are quite enjoyable in themselves, there is an often neglected serious side to *Rocky Horror*. If one doubts the presence of this quiet sincerity at the center of the film, admittedly clothed quite elaborately within a shield of detached, reflexive self-awareness, for one example recall the look on Columbia's (Nell Campbell) face after Frank-N-Furter has finished his closing "explanation" for his actions, the melancholic torch song "I'm Going Home," as he bows and raises his hands in fragile acknowledgment of the applause from an audience which exists only in his mind.

The suggestively sad power of the film is that it refuses to offer simple answers as to how an individual's deep feeling of "difference" can be readily made sense of, and how deep the pain may go. As Brad (Barry Bostwick) says in the concluding song "Super Heroes," cut from the U.S. version of the film, "to find the truth, I've even lied, but all I know is down inside I'm bleeding." The film acts to reassure fans of the acceptability of their own sense of difference yet also continually works to remind them of that very difference.

Speaking to this dichotomy are comments made by both Susan Sarandon, who plays ingénue Janet Weiss, and Richard O'Brien, writer of the original stage musical who also plays the part of the sinister Riff-Raff. Sarandon offers an assessment of the film's appeal by saying that "whatever the movie says, especially to lonely kids," it offers a kind of liberation, a way to act out, in a sense, and become part of a new kind of community. And yet, as O'Brien indicates, the ending of the film may provide a catharsis, but as to what kind of release it may ultimately prove to be, he doesn't know, as to Brad and Janet, will what they have been through "scar them for life or bring them joy?"

The film strikes a very successful balance between these two positions. At once a parodic reenactment of an earlier genre of horror and science fiction cinema, which more often than not displayed the RKO Studios radio tower before their dark little morality plays, and a rock musical developed out of a successful and popular stage production, *Rocky Horror* represents the intersection point of odd bedfellows. Richard O'Brien's musical has strangeness in its very bones thanks to the offbeat materials with which he chose to build his monster. The film re-creates the unsettling plasticity of 1950s horror/sci-fi movies perfectly, and by combining the often overtly mannered and stiff style of those films to the reflexive sensibility of an absurdist theatricality, the result is a comedic yet ever so slightly, perhaps almost unconsciously, disturbing hybrid, neither one thing nor another, an eccentric wind-up toy unearthed from some other place and time.

O'Brien's music is both celebratorially campy and bizarrely sublime, ranging from the dementedly joyous rock charms of "The Time Warp" and "Sweet Transvestite" to the bubbly pop of "Touch Me" to the melodramatically self-aware and yet no less melancholic reflection of the aforementioned "I'm Going Home." All of the music exists in a kind of multi-temporal void which further woks to generate the curious "otherness" of the film, combining bits of Broadway reverie and swells with pop and rock anthems from the 1950s and 70s, all evoking the spirit of a sideshow attraction. Presented like a retro artifact, but one seemingly designed after a glance back from some distant future, the film is paste boarded in popping comic book colors and a strikingly bubble-gum gothic décor seeping a garishly urgent and desperate sexuality.

Rocky Horror not only calls attention to its own materiality by way of its mise-en-scene, one part carnivalesque parade and one part soft-core sex flick, but also by the constant breaking of the dramatic fourth wall. It's no wonder audiences began to yell back at the screen after *Rocky Horror*'s release; the film initiates that dialogue by positioning characters as capable of acknowledging the audience, often addressing viewers with a line of commentary or even a knowing look or raised eyebrow. Indeed, the line of dialogue that begins this review is spoken directly to the camera by Frank-N-Furter as if it was a private moment not to be shared with anyone save the mad doctor and his intimate listeners. Charles Grey's Criminologist narrator is perhaps the most explicit example of this nod to the viewer that is the equivalent of a shared wink, an acknowledgment of artifice which, by heightening the film's reflexivity, makes the narrative's serious turns all the more poignant. This intimacy between character and viewer can only really succeed, however, when the performative aspect of the work rises beyond mere cliché.

The roles in *Rocky Horror* are meant to be parodically stereotyped in their broad outlines, but the story, as a series of unfolding revelations both personal and narrative, reveals levels of inner dimensions. The end result is that the film could best be described as one costume party being held within another, a kind of elaborately staged play being performed within the narrative framework of a larger film, wherein a layering of character has a chance to occur. Characters who initially appear to be one-dimensional cutouts eventually shed their costuming, usually quite literally, and reveal something more underneath, an endless removal of masks that doesn't seem to end with any clear sense of finality, like a spiraling progression of ever shrinking Russian dolls, each within the body of the next. This depth of character is not merely a narrative contrivance but stems from purposeful intent on the part of the performances, with two in particular standing out, Sarandon as Janet and Tim Curry as Frank-N-Furter.

As described by Sarandon, Janet was in a way a "take off on myself," or more precisely a *"Saturday Night Live* version of all the roles I had been playing" up to that point. "You scratch one of those ingénues, there's a bitch somewhere," she remarks. Sarandon plays Janet, one of the most intentionally one-dimensional of the stereotypes at the film's beginning, by being honest even to her character's woodenness, by making that cliché feel more like the result of the repression of an inner life rather than propping Janet up as merely a thing to laugh at. The character's transformation, her awakening into something more of herself, is as comically precise as it is organically developed. Sarandon comments on the DVD release that she was "brave enough and stupid enough" to go with things that crossed her path and seems quite sanguine with her role as Janet, remarking that "it will be the *Rocky Horror* show that is in the time capsule" out of all her films.

And perhaps this wouldn't be such a terrible thing ultimately, for if actors can perform at their best in even the so-called "B" grade productions, then it speaks highly of them. This is particularly true of Tim Curry who is spellbinding at Frank-N-Furter, a role he had already quite snugly steeled into during the stage production. Curry camps without undercutting and sneers without being superior, investing an emotional substance in the film while juggling with its essential nature as a comedic parody, finding the perfect balance between outrageous peacocking and surprising fragility.

This duality could be applied to the film as a whole. Yet this is not to suggest that what is at work in the film is the profoundest of explorations of human identity; *Rocky Horror* is first and foremost a demented comedy, a musical trip down a particular cinematic memory lane, and an entertaining one at that. But it can be revealing to look more closely at a film that has been somewhat simplified in its reception by the theatrical displays of its fandom. This is not to suggest that they are necessarily missing something but that the film does indeed operate at more levels than may seem readily apparent amid all the spectacle.

Joe (1970)
by Ryan Cracknell (for ReelTalk Movie Reviews)

In 1970, America was in a state of flux. The Baby Boomers were coming of age, and their parents were stuck in a cultural gap. The Liberal hippie movement was making noise while the old Conservative guard was left to complain and reminisce about the good old days of drive-ins and the Twist. Filmmaker John G. Avildsen traces this transition period of changing moral values in *Joe*, a heavy-handed commentary on the past and then-present colliding.

Today, *Joe* is most notable for the debut of Susan Sarandon. She plays Melissa, a hippie rejecting her materialistic upbringing. Although her role is limited, Melissa's innocent lost-lamb persona is the driving force of the entire film. Her wealthy father, Bill Compton (Dennis Patrick), still views his daughter as a child. He sees it as his duty to protect his daughter. When Melissa ends up in the hospital from an overdose, Bill feels like a failure. He goes back to Melissa's flat where he fights with her drug-dealing boyfriend. Bill ends up with blood on his hands; Melissa runs away; and Bill's conscience returns.

Along comes Joe (Peter Boyle), a pig-headed bigot if there ever was one. In Joe's narrow-minded world, intolerance is called patriotism. He wants America to stay the same. In fact, his racist opinions make you believe that given the option, Joe would rather live in the times when he could relax on a cotton farm and have slaves do all his work.

Bill and Joe make an unlikely pair but a pair nonetheless. They head out onto the streets of New York looking for Melissa. What their search actually does is give Joe a chance to encounter his greatest fears head-on as they run into all sorts of hippies, Liberals and other sorts looking to give America a modern and more tolerant attitude.

Joe hasn't aged well. It's a celluloid time capsule that effectively captures 1970 America in its look and sound, but the themes don't transfer well at all. The then Liberal movement has become a way of life, and guys like Joe are left sipping Canadian Club on their rickety porches with a tattered American flag blowing in the wind above them.

Norman Wexler's screenplay is as subtle as a fourth of July fireworks display. He hammers his message of cultural divide relying primarily on Joe's strong and distinct voice. Of course, you hate Joe—but that's not the point. He's so delusional you can't help feeling sorry for him.

It's interesting to see the beginning of Sarandon's career and how she ended up a Liberal free spirit right off the bat. She plays much more the victim than she would in later years, but it's a start. The role of Melissa isn't one of Sarandon's most challenging, although it does provide a couple of opportunities for her to shine. Her small, doe-eyed appearance is perfect to reflect the lost innocence not only of Melissa but of America as a whole. As a young adult, Melissa was meant to symbolize the future by providing a warning about what would happen if the country's attitude continued to reflect through people like Joe.

Difficult as it is not to laugh at *Joe* today, this film shows the different faces of one's love of country. And like Bill, who couldn't handle his daughter growing up, sometimes you have to let your own memories of a loved one go in order to allow them to grow. (Released by MGM/UA Studios and rated "R.")

ABOUT THE AUTHOR

"All I know is what I see in the movies," Betty Jo Tucker insists. Because of a passion for film, Betty Jo and her husband Larry see almost 200 movies a year. A retired college dean, Betty Jo currently serves as lead critic for ReelTalk Movie Reviews (www.reeltalkreviews.com) and writes film commentary for News First Online (an NBC-affiliate website) and the *Colorado Senior Beacon*.

Phil Hall, book editor for the *New York Resident*, calls Betty Jo one of the Internet's finest film critics and "a graceful, intelligent judge of cinematic offerings." According to Hall, "Tucker is wonderful as an observer and cogent as an interviewer. She approaches her subject with measured dignity (when the efforts are unsatisfactory) and mature enthusiasm (when the efforts are deemed worthy)." Regarding her interviews, Hall says, "Whether dealing with art-house deities or popcorn favorites, Tucker is blessed with knowing how to ask the right questions and how to steer a conversation in unexpected directions."

During her seven years as an entertainment journalist, Betty Jo has interviewed such stars and filmmakers as Ian McKellen, Brendan Fraser, Angelina Jolie, Guy Pearce, Aidan Quinn, Phillip Noyce, Tony Shalhoub, Chen Kaige, Aaron Eckhart, Willem Dafoe, Oliver Parker, Douglas McGrath, Hector Elizondo, and Annette Bening.

While serving as Dean of Humanities at San Diego Mesa College, Betty Jo supervised expansion of the film studies curriculum, designed an "Exploring Human Values through Film" course, and coordinated the "Reel to Real Film Forum" program.

Betty Jo helped found the San Diego Film Critics Society and is a member of the Online Film Critics Society. Her amusing life-at-the-movies memoir, *Confessions of a Movie Addict* (Hats Off Books, 2001), has received rave reviews from film fans and critics alike. "If Oscars were given out for the funniest book of the year, *Confessions of a Movie Addict* would win hands down," writes James Colt Harrison, editor of *National PreVue Film Magazine*. Scott Smith, "Lifestyle" reporter for the *Pueblo Chieftain*, calls Betty Jo's movie memoir "chatty, funny and overflowing with all things cinematic—just like the author."

Betty Jo and Larry (who, writing as Harry and Elizabeth Lawrence, co-authored *It Had To Be Us*, a romantic memoir selected by SANDS Publishing as one of its inaugural offerings in 2001) enjoy spending time with their son and daughter and seven grand-children—who also love movies. The Tuckers live—where else—just five minutes away from Tinseltown, the only multiplex theater in Pueblo, Colorado.

INDICES

Images/Photographs:

Movies

147

People

Plays:

CPSIA information can be obtained
at www.ICGtesting.com
Printed in the USA
LVHW112227271021
701762LV00005B/113

9 781587 363009